The Silverado Squatters

Robert Louis Stevenson

Contents

THE SILVERADO SQUATTERS

BY

Robert Louis Stevenson

THE SILVERADO SQUATTERS

The scene of this little book is on a high mountain. There are, indeed, many higher; there are many of a nobler outline. It is no place of pilgrimage for the summary globe-trotter; but to one who lives upon its sides, Mount Saint Helena soon becomes a centre of interest. It is the Mont Blanc of one section of the Californian Coast Range, none of its near neighbours rising to one-half its altitude. It looks down on much green, intricate country. It feeds in the spring-time many splashing brooks. From its summit you must have an excellent lesson of geography: seeing, to the south, San Francisco Bay, with Tamalpais on the one hand and Monte Diablo on the other; to the west and thirty miles away, the open ocean; eastward, across the corn-lands and thick tule swamps of Sacramento Valley, to where the Central Pacific railroad begins to climb the sides of the Sierras; and northward, for what I know, the white head of Shasta looking down on Oregon. Three counties, Napa County, Lake County, and Sonoma County, march across its cliffy shoulders. Its naked peak stands nearly four thousand five hundred feet above the sea; its sides are fringed with forest; and the soil, where it is bare, glows warm with cinnabar.

Life in its shadow goes rustically forward. Bucks, and bears, and rattle-snakes, and former mining operations, are the staple of men's talk. Agriculture has only begun to mount above the valley. And though in a few years from now the whole district may be smiling with farms, passing trains shaking the mountain to the heart, many-windowed hotels lighting up the night like factories, and a prosperous city occupying the site of sleepy Calistoga; yet in the mean time, around the foot of that mountain the silence of nature reigns in a great measure unbroken, and the people of hill and valley go sauntering about their business as in the days before the flood.

To reach Mount Saint Helena from San Francisco, the traveller has twice to cross the bay: once by the busy Oakland Ferry, and again, after an hour or so of the railway, from Vallejo junction to Vallejo. Thence he takes rail once more to mount the long green strath of Napa Valley.

In all the contractions and expansions of that inland sea, the Bay of San Francisco, there can be few drearier scenes than the Vallejo Ferry. Bald shores and a low, bald islet inclose the sea; through the narrows the tide bubbles, muddy like a river. When we made the passage (bound, although yet we knew it not, for Silverado) the steamer jumped, and the black buoys were dancing in the jabble; the ocean breeze blew killing chill; and, although the upper sky was still unflecked with vapour, the sea fogs were pouring in from seaward, over the hilltops of Marin county, in one great, shapeless, silver cloud.

South Vallejo is typical of many Californian towns. It was a blunder; the site has proved untenable; and, although it is still such a young place by the scale of Europe, it has already begun to be deserted for its neighbour and namesake, North Vallejo. A long pier, a number of drinking saloons, a hotel of a great size, marshy pools where the frogs keep up their croaking, and even at high noon the entire absence of any human face or voice--these are the marks of South Vallejo. Yet there was a tall building beside the pier, labelled the Star Flour Mills; and sea-going, full-rigged ships lay close along shore, waiting for their cargo. Soon these would be plunging round the Horn, soon the flour from the Star Flour Mills would be landed on the wharves of Liverpool. For that, too, is one of England's outposts; thither, to this gaunt mill, across the Atlantic and Pacific deeps and round about the icy Horn, this crowd of great, three-masted, deep-sea ships come, bringing nothing, and return with bread.

The Frisby House, for that was the name of the hotel, was a place of fallen fortunes, like the town. It was now given up to labourers, and partly ruinous. At dinner there was the ordinary display of what is called in the west a TWO-BIT HOUSE: the tablecloth checked red and white, the plague of flies, the wire hencoops over the dishes, the great variety and invariable vileness of the food and the rough coatless men devoting it in silence. In our bedroom, the stove would not burn, though it would smoke; and while one window would not open, the other would not shut. There was a view on a bit of empty road, a few dark houses, a donkey wandering with its shadow on a slope, and a blink of sea, with a tall ship lying anchored in the moonlight. All about that dreary inn frogs sang their ungainly chorus.

Early the next morning we mounted the hill along a wooden footway, bridging one marish spot after another. Here and there, as we ascended, we passed a house embowered in white roses. More of the bay became apparent, and soon the blue peak of Tamalpais rose above the green level of the island opposite. It told us we were still but a little way from the city of the Golden Gates, already, at that hour, beginning to awake among the sand-hills. It called to us over the waters as with the voice of a bird. Its stately head, blue as a sapphire on the paler azure of the sky, spoke to us of wider outlooks and the bright Pacific. For Tamalpais stands sentry, like a lighthouse, over the Golden Gates, between the bay and the open ocean, and looks down indifferently on both. Even as we saw and hailed it from Vallejo, sea-men, far out at sea, were scanning it with shaded eyes; and, as if to answer to the thought, one of the great ships below began silently to clothe herself with white sails, homeward bound for England.

For some way beyond Vallejo the railway led us through bald green pastures. On the west the rough highlands of Marin shut off the ocean; in the midst, in long, straggling, gleaming arms, the bay died out among the grass; there were few trees and few enclosures; the sun shone wide over open uplands, the displumed hills stood clear against the sky. But by-and-by these hills began to draw nearer on either hand, and first thicket and then wood began to clothe their sides; and soon we were away from all signs of the sea's neighbourhood, mounting an inland, irrigated valley. A great variety of oaks stood, now severally, now in a becoming grove, among the fields and vineyards. The towns were compact, in about equal proportions, of bright, new wooden houses and great and growing forest trees; and the chapel bell on the engine sounded most festally that sunny Sunday, as we drew up at one green town after another, with the townsfolk trooping in their Sunday's best to see the strangers, with the sun sparkling on the clean houses, and great domes of foliage humming overhead in the breeze.

This pleasant Napa Valley is, at its north end, blockaded by our mountain. There, at Calistoga, the railroad ceases, and the traveller who intends faring farther, to the Geysers or to the springs in Lake County, must cross the spurs of the mountain by stage. Thus, Mount Saint Helena is not only a summit, but a frontier; and, up to the time of writing, it has stayed the progress of the iron horse.

PART I--IN THE VALLEY

CHAPTER I--CALISTOGA

It is difficult for a European to imagine Calistoga, the whole place is so new, and of such an accidental pattern; the very name, I hear, was invented at a supper-party by the man who found the springs.

The railroad and the highway come up the valley about parallel to one another. The street of Calistoga joins the perpendicular to both--a wide street, with bright, clean, low houses, here and there a verandah over the sidewalk, here and there a horse-post, here and there lounging townsfolk. Other streets are marked out, and most likely named; for these towns in the New World begin with a firm resolve to grow larger, Washington and Broadway, and then First and Second, and so forth, being boldly plotted out as soon as the community indulges in a plan. But, in the meanwhile, all the life and most of the houses of Calistoga are concentrated upon that street between the railway station and the road. I never heard it called by any name, but I will hazard a guess that it is either Washington or Broadway. Here are the blacksmith's, the chemist's, the general merchant's, and Kong Sam Kee, the Chinese laundryman's; here, probably, is the office of the local paper (for the place has a paper--they all have papers); and here certainly is one of the hotels, Cheeseborough's, whence the daring Foss, a man dear to legend, starts his horses for the Geysers.

It must be remembered that we are here in a land of stage-drivers and highwaymen: a land, in that sense, like England a hundred years ago. The highway robber--road-agent, he is quaintly called-- is still busy in these parts. The fame of Vasquez is still young. Only a few years go, the Lakeport stage was robbed a mile or two from Calistoga. In 1879, the dentist of Mendocino City, fifty miles away upon the coast, suddenly threw off the garments of his trade, like Grindoff, in The Miller and his Men, and flamed forth in his second dress as a captain of banditti. A great robbery was followed by a long chase, a chase of days if not of weeks, among the intricate hill-country; and the chase was followed by much desultory fighting, in which several--and the dentist, I believe, amongst the number--bit the dust. The grass was springing for the first time, nourished upon their blood, when I arrived in Calistoga. I am reminded of another highwayman of that same year. "He had been unwell," so ran his humorous defence, "and the doctor told him to take something, so he took the express-box."

The cultus of the stage-coachman always flourishes highest where there are thieves on the road, and where the guard travels armed, and the stage is not only a link between country and city, and the vehicle of news, but has a faint warfaring aroma, like a man who should be brother to a soldier. California boasts her famous stage-drivers, and among the famous Foss is not forgotten. Along the unfenced, abominable mountain roads, he launches his team with small regard to human life or the doctrine of probabilities. Flinching travellers, who behold themselves coasting eternity at every corner, look with natural admiration at their driver's huge, impassive, fleshy countenance. He has the very face for the driver in Sam Weller's anecdote, who upset the election party at the required point. Wonderful tales are current of his readiness and skill. One in particular, of how one of his horses fell at a ticklish passage of the road, and how Foss let slip the reins, and, driving over the fallen animal, arrived at the next stage with only three. This I relate as I heard it, without guarantee.

I only saw Foss once, though, strange as it may sound, I have twice talked with him. He lives out of Calistoga, at a ranche called Fossville. One evening, after he was long gone home, I dropped into Cheeseborough's, and was asked if I should like to speak with Mr. Foss. Supposing that the interview was impossible, and that I was merely called upon to subscribe the general sentiment, I boldly answered "Yes." Next moment, I had one instrument at my ear, another at my mouth and found myself, with nothing in the world to say, conversing with a man several miles off among desolate hills. Foss rapidly and somewhat plaintively brought the conversation to an end; and he returned to his night's grog at Fossville, while I strolled forth again on Calistoga high street. But it was an odd thing that here, on what we are accustomed to consider the very skirts of civilization, I should have used the telephone for the first time in my civilized career. So it goes in these young countries; telephones, and telegraphs, and newspapers, and advertisements running far ahead among the Indians and the grizzly bears.

Alone, on the other side of the railway, stands the Springs Hotel, with its attendant cottages. The floor of the valley is extremely level to the very roots of the hills; only here and there a hillock, crowned with pines, rises like the barrow of some chieftain famed in war; and right against one of these hillocks is the Springs Hotel--is or was; for since I was there the place has been destroyed by fire, and has risen again from its ashes. A lawn runs about the house, and the lawn is in its turn surrounded by a system of little five-roomed cottages, each with a verandah and a weedy palm before the door. Some of the cottages are let to residents, and these are wreathed in flowers. The rest are occupied by ordinary visitors to the Hotel; and a very pleasant way this is, by which you have a little country cottage of your own, without domestic burthens, and by the day or week.

The whole neighbourhood of Mount Saint Helena is full of sulphur and of boiling springs. The Geysers are famous; they were the great health resort of the Indians before the coming of the whites. Lake County is dotted with spas; Hot Springs and White Sulphur Springs are the names of two stations on the Napa Valley railroad; and Calistoga itself seems to repose on a mere film above a boiling, subterranean lake. At one end of the hotel enclosure are the springs from which it takes its name, hot enough to scald a child seriously while I was there. At the other end, the tenant of a cottage sank a well, and there also the water came up boiling. It keeps this end of the valley as warm as a toast. I have gone across to the hotel a little after five in the morning, when a sea fog from the Pacific was hanging thick and gray, and dark and dirty overhead, and found the thermometer had been up before me, and had already climbed among the nineties; and in the stress of the day it was sometimes too hot to move about.

But in spite of this heat from above and below, doing one on both sides, Calistoga was a pleasant place to dwell in; beautifully green, for it was then that favoured moment in the Californian year, when the rains are over and the dusty summer has not yet set in; often visited by fresh airs, now from the mountain, now across

Sonoma from the sea; very quiet, very idle, very silent but for the breezes and the cattle bells afield. And there was something satisfactory in the sight of that great mountain that enclosed us to the north: whether it stood, robed in sunshine, quaking to its topmost pinnacle with the heat and brightness of the day; or whether it set itself to weaving vapours, wisp after wisp growing, trembling, fleeting, and fading in the blue.

The tangled, woody, and almost trackless foot-hills that enclose the valley, shutting it off from Sonoma on the west, and from Yolo on the east--rough as they were in outline, dug out by winter streams, crowned by cliffy bluffs and nodding pine trees--wore dwarfed into satellites by the bulk and bearing of Mount Saint Helena. She over-towered them by two-thirds of her own stature. She excelled them by the boldness of her profile. Her great bald summit, clear of trees and pasture, a cairn of quartz and cinnabar, rejected kinship with the dark and shaggy wilderness of lesser hill-tops.

CHAPTER II--THE PETRIFIED FOREST

We drove off from the Springs Hotel about three in the afternoon. The sun warmed me to the heart. A broad, cool wind streamed pauselessly down the valley, laden with perfume. Up at the top stood Mount Saint Helena, a bulk of mountain, bare atop, with tree-fringed spurs, and radiating warmth. Once we saw it framed in a grove of tall and exquisitely graceful white oaks, in line and colour a finished composition. We passed a cow stretched by the roadside, her bell slowly beating time to the movement of her ruminating jaws, her big red face crawled over by half a dozen flies, a monument of content.

A little farther, and we struck to the left up a mountain road, and for two hours threaded one valley after another, green, tangled, full of noble timber, giving us every now and again a sight of Mount Saint Helena and the blue hilly distance, and crossed by many streams, through which we splashed to the carriage-step. To the right or the left, there was scarce any trace of man but the road we followed; I think we passed but oneranchero's house in the whole distance, and that was closed and smokeless. But we had the society of these bright streams--dazzlingly clear, as is their wont, splashing from the wheels in diamonds, and striking a lively coolness through the sunshine. And what with the innumerable variety of greens, the masses of foliage tossing in the breeze, the glimpses of distance, the descents into seemingly impenetrable thickets, the continual dodging of the road which made haste to plunge again into the covert, we had a fine sense of woods, and spring-time, and the open air.

Our driver gave me a lecture by the way on Californian trees--a thing I was much in need of, having fallen among painters who know the name of nothing, and Mexicans who know the name of nothing in English. He taught me the madrona, the manzanita, the buck-eye, the maple; he showed me the crested mountain quail; he showed me where some young redwoods were already spiring heavenwards from the ruins of the old; for in this district all had already perished: redwoods and redskins, the two noblest indigenous living things, alike condemned.

At length, in a lonely dell, we came on a huge wooden gate with a sign upon it like an inn. "The Petrified Forest. Proprietor: C. Evans," ran the legend. Within, on a knoll of sward, was the house of the proprietor, and another smaller house hard by to serve as a museum, where photographs and petrifactions were retailed. It was a pure little isle of touristry among these solitary hills.

The proprietor was a brave old white-faced Swede. He had wandered this way, Heaven knows how, and taken up his acres--I forget how many years ago--all alone, bent double with sciatica, and with six bits in his pocket and an axe upon his shoulder. Long, useless years of seafaring had thus discharged him at the end, penniless and sick. Without doubt he had tried his luck at the diggings, and got no good from that; without doubt he had loved the bottle, and lived the life of Jack ashore. But at the end of these adventures, here he came; and, the place hitting his fancy, down he sat to make a new life of it, far from crimps and the salt sea. And the very sight of his ranche had done him good. It was "the handsomest spot in the Californy mountains." "Isn't it handsome, now?" he said. Every penny he makes goes into that ranche to make it handsomer. Then the climate, with the sea-breeze every afternoon in the hottest summer weather, had gradually cured the sciatica; and his sister and niece were now domesticated with him for company--or, rather, the niece came only once in the two days, teaching music the meanwhile in the valley. And then, for a last piece of luck, "the handsomest spot in the Californy mountains" had produced a petrified forest, which Mr. Evans now shows at the modest figure of half a dollar a head, or two-thirds of his capital when he first came there with an axe and a sciatica.

This tardy favourite of fortune--hobbling a little, I think, as if in memory of the sciatica, but with not a trace that I can remember of the sea--thoroughly ruralized from head to foot, proceeded to escort us up the hill behind his house.

"Who first found the forest?" asked my wife.

"The first? I was that man," said he. "I was cleaning up the pasture for my beasts, when I found THIS"--kicking a great redwood seven feet in diameter, that lay there on its side, hollow heart, clinging lumps of bark, all changed into gray stone, with veins of quartz between what had been the layers of the wood.

"Were you surprised?"

"Surprised? No! What would I be surprised about? What did I know about petrifactions--following the sea? Petrifaction! There was no such word in my language! I knew about putrifaction, though! I thought it was a stone; so would you, if you was cleaning up pasture."

And now he had a theory of his own, which I did not quite grasp, except that the trees had not "grewed" there. But he mentioned, with evident pride, that he differed from all the scientific people who had visited the spot; and he flung about such words as "tufa" and "scilica" with careless freedom.

When I mentioned I was from Scotland, "My old country," he said; "my old country"--with a smiling look and a tone of real affection in his voice. I was mightily surprised, for he was obviously Scandinavian, and begged him to explain. It seemed he had learned his English and done nearly all his sailing in Scotch ships. "Out of Glasgow," said he, "or Greenock; but that's all the same--they all hail from Glasgow." And he was so pleased with me for being a Scotsman, and his adopted compatriot, that he made me a present of a very beautiful piece of petrifaction--I believe the most beautiful and portable he had.

Here was a man, at least, who was a Swede, a Scot, and an American, acknowledging some kind allegiance to three lands. Mr. Wallace's Scoto-Circassian will not fail to come before the reader. I have myself met and spoken with a Fifeshire German, whose combination of abominable accents struck me dumb. But, indeed, I think we all belong to many countries. And perhaps this habit of much travel, and the engendering of scattered friendships, may prepare the euthanasia of ancient nations.

And the forest itself? Well, on a tangled, briery hillside--for the pasture would bear a little further cleaning up, to my eyes-- there lie scattered thickly various lengths of petrified trunk, such as the one already mentioned. It is very curious, of course, and ancient enough, if that were all. Doubtless, the heart of the geologist beats quicker at the sight; but, for my part, I was mightily unmoved. Sight-seeing is the art of disappointment.

"There's nothing under heaven so blue, That's fairly worth the travelling to."

But, fortunately, Heaven rewards us with many agreeable prospects and adventures by the way; and sometimes, when we go out to see a petrified forest, prepares a far more delightful curiosity, in the form of Mr. Evans, whom may all prosperity attend throughout a long and green old age.

CHAPTER III--NAPA WINE

I was interested in Californian wine. Indeed, I am interested in all wines, and have been all my life, from the raisin wine that a schoolfellow kept secreted in his play-box up to my last discovery, those notable Valtellines, that once shone upon the board of Caesar.

Some of us, kind old Pagans, watch with dread the shadows falling on the age: how the unconquerable worm invades the sunny terraces of France, and Bordeaux is no more, and the Rhone a mere Arabia Petraea. Chateau Neuf is dead, and I have never tasted it; Hermitage--a hermitage indeed from all life's sorrows--lies expiring by the river. And in the place of these imperial elixirs, beautiful to every sense, gem-hued, flower-scented, dream- compellers:- behold upon the quays at Cette the chemicals arrayed; behold the analyst at Marseilles, raising hands in obsecration, attesting god Lyoeus, and the vats staved in, and the dishonest wines poured forth among the sea. It is not Pan only; Bacchus, too, is dead.

If wine is to withdraw its most poetic countenance, the sun of the white dinner-cloth, a deity to be invoked by two or three, all fervent, hushing their talk, degusting tenderly, and storing reminiscences--for a bottle of good wine, like a good act, shines ever in the retrospect--if wine is to desert us, go thy ways, old Jack! Now we begin to have compunctions, and look back at the brave bottles squandered upon dinner-parties, where the guests drank grossly, discussing politics the while, and even the schoolboy "took his whack," like liquorice water. And at the same time, we look timidly forward, with a spark of hope, to where the new lands, already weary of producing gold, begin to green with vineyards. A nice point in human history falls to be decided by Californian and Australian wines.

Wine in California is still in the experimental stage; and when you taste a vintage, grave economical questions are involved. The beginning of vine-planting is like the beginning of mining for the precious metals: the wine-grower also "Prospects." One corner of land after another is tried with one kind of grape after another. This is a failure; that is better; a third best. So, bit by bit, they grope about for their Clos Vougeot and Lafite. Those lodes and pockets of earth, more precious than the precious ores, that yield inimitable fragrance and soft fire; those virtuous Bonanzas, where the soil has sublimated under sun and stars to something finer, and the wine is bottled poetry: these still lie undiscovered; chaparral conceals, thicket embowers them; the miner chips the rock and wanders farther, and the grizzly muses undisturbed. But there they bide their hour, awaiting their Columbus; and nature nurses and prepares them. The smack of Californian earth shall linger on the palate of your grandson.

Meanwhile the wine is merely a good wine; the best that I have tasted better than a Beaujolais, and not unlike. But the trade is poor; it lives from hand to mouth, putting its all into experiments, and forced to sell its vintages. To find one properly matured, and bearing its own name, is to be fortune's favourite.

Bearing its own name, I say, and dwell upon the innuendo.

"You want to know why California wine is not drunk in the States?" a San Francisco wine merchant said to me, after he had shown me through his premises. "Well, here's the reason."

And opening a large cupboard, fitted with many little drawers, he proceeded to shower me all over with a great variety of gorgeously tinted labels, blue, red, or yellow, stamped with crown or coronet, and hailing from such a profusion of clos and chateaux, that a single department could scarce have furnished forth the names. But it was strange that all looked unfamiliar.

"Chateau X-?" said I. "I never heard of that."

"I dare say not," said he. "I had been reading one of X-'s novels."

They were all castles in Spain! But that sure enough is the reason why California wine is not drunk in the States.

Napa valley has been long a seat of the wine-growing industry. It did not here begin, as it does too often, in the low valley lands along the river, but took at once to the rough foot-hills, where alone it can expect to prosper. A basking inclination, and stones, to be a reservoir of the day's heat, seem necessary to the soil for wine; the grossness of the earth must be evaporated, its marrow daily melted and refined for ages; until at length these clods that break below our footing, and to the eye appear but common earth, are truly and to the perceiving mind, a masterpiece of nature. The dust of Richebourg, which the wind carries away, what an apotheosis of the dust! Not man himself can seem a stranger child of that brown, friable powder, than the blood and sun in that old flask behind the faggots.

A Californian vineyard, one of man's outposts in the wilderness, has features of its own. There is nothing here to remind you of the Rhine or Rhone, of the low cote d'or, or the infamous and scabby deserts of Champagne; but all is green, solitary, covert. We visited two of them, Mr. Schram's and Mr. M'Eckron's, sharing the same glen.

Some way down the valley below Calistoga, we turned sharply to the south and plunged into the thick of the wood. A rude trail rapidly mounting; a little stream tinkling by on the one hand, big enough perhaps after the rains, but already yielding up its life; overhead and on all sides a bower of green and tangled thicket, still fragrant and still flower-bespangled by the early season, where thimble-berry played the part of our English hawthorn, and the buck-eyes were putting forth their twisted horns of blossom: through all this, we struggled toughly upwards, canted to and fro by the roughness of the trail, and continually switched across the face by sprays of leaf or blossom. The last is no great inconvenience at home; but here in California it is a matter of some moment. For in all woods and by every wayside there prospers an abominable shrub or weed, called poison-oak, whose very neighbourhood is venomous to some, and whose actual touch is avoided by the most impervious.

The two houses, with their vineyards, stood each in a green niche of its own in this steep and narrow forest dell. Though they were so near, there was already a good difference in level; and Mr. M'Eckron's head must be a long way under the feet of Mr. Schram. No more had been cleared than was necessary for cultivation; close around each oasis ran the tangled wood; the glen enfolds them; there they lie basking in sun and silence, concealed from all but the clouds and the mountain birds.

Mr. M'Eckron's is a bachelor establishment; a little bit of a wooden house, a small cellar hard by in the hillside, and a patch of vines planted and tended single-handed by himself. He had but recently began; his vines were young, his business young also; but I thought he had the look of the man who succeeds. He hailed from Greenock: he remembered his father putting him inside Mons Meg, and that touched me home; and we exchanged a word or two of Scotch, which pleased me more than you would fancy.

Mr. Schram's, on the other hand, is the oldest vineyard in the valley, eighteen years old, I think; yet he began a penniless barber, and even after he had broken ground up here with his black malvoisies, continued for long to tramp the valley with his razor. Now, his place is the picture of prosperity: stuffed birds in the verandah, cellars far dug into the hillside, and resting on pillars like a bandit's cave:- all trimness, varnish, flowers, and sunshine, among the tangled wildwood. Stout, smiling Mrs. Schram, who has been to Europe and apparently all about the States for pleasure, entertained Fanny in the verandah, while I was tasting wines in the cellar. To Mr. Schram this was a solemn office; his serious gusto warmed my heart; prosperity had not yet wholly banished a certain neophite and girlish trepidation, and he followed every sip and read my face with proud anxiety. I tasted all. I tasted every variety and shade of Schramberger, red and white Schramberger, Burgundy Schramberger, Schramberger Hock, Schramberger Golden Chasselas, the latter with a notable bouquet, and I fear to think how many more. Much of it goes to London-- most, I think; and Mr. Schram has a great notion of the English taste.

In this wild spot, I did not feel the sacredness of ancient cultivation. It was still raw, it was no Marathon, and no Johannisberg; yet the stirring sunlight, and the growing vines, and the vats and bottles in the cavern, made a pleasant music for the mind. Here, also, earth's cream was being skimmed and garnered; and the London customers can taste, such as it is, the tang of the earth in this green valley. So local, so quintessential is a wine, that it seems the very birds in the verandah might communicate a flavour, and that romantic cellar influence the bottle next to be uncorked in Pimlico, and the smile of jolly Mr. Schram might mantle in the glass.

But these are but experiments. All things in this new land are moving farther on: the wine-vats and the miner's blasting tools but picket for a night, like Bedouin pavillions; and to-morrow, to fresh woods! This stir of change and these perpetual echoes of the moving footfall, haunt the land. Men move eternally, still chasing Fortune; and, fortune found, still wander. As we drove back to Calistoga, the road lay empty of mere passengers, but its green side was dotted with the camps of travelling families: one cumbered with a great waggonful of household stuff, settlers going to occupy a ranche they had taken up in Mendocino, or perhaps Tehama County; another, a party in dust coats, men and women, whom we found camped in a grove on the roadside, all on pleasure bent, with a Chinaman to cook for them, and who waved their hands to us as we drove by.

CHAPTER IV--THE SCOT ABROAD

A few pages back, I wrote that a man belonged, in these days, to a variety of countries; but the old land is still the true love, the others are but pleasant infidelities. Scotland is indefinable; it has no unity except upon the map. Two languages, many dialects, innumerable forms of piety, and countless local patriotisms and prejudices, part us among ourselves more widely than the extreme east and west of that great continent of America. When I am at home, I feel a man from Glasgow to be something like a rival, a man from Barra to be more than half a foreigner. Yet let us meet in some far country, and, whether we hail from the braes of Manor or the braes of Mar, some ready-made affection joins us on the instant. It is not race. Look at us. One is Norse, one Celtic, and another Saxon. It is not community of tongue. We have it not among ourselves; and we have it almost to perfection, with English, or Irish, or American. It is no tie of faith, for we detest each other's errors. And yet somewhere, deep down in the heart of each one of us, something yearns for the old land, and the old kindly people.

Of all mysteries of the human heart, this is perhaps the most inscrutable. There is no special loveliness in that gray country, with its rainy, sea-beat archipelago; its fields of dark mountains; its unsightly places, black with coal; its treeless, sour, unfriendly looking corn-lands; its quaint, gray, castled city, where the bells clash of a Sunday, and the wind squalls, and the salt showers fly and beat. I do not even know if I desire to live there; but let me hear, in some far land, a kindred voice sing out, "Oh, why left I my hame?" and it seems at once as if no beauty under the kind heavens, and no society of the wise and good, can repay me for my absence from my country. And though I think I would rather die elsewhere, yet in my heart of hearts I long to be buried among good Scots clods. I will say it fairly, it grows on me with every year: there are no stars so lovely as Edinburgh street-lamps. When

I forget thee, auld Reekie, may my right hand forget its cunning!

The happiest lot on earth is to be born a Scotchman. You must pay for it in many ways, as for all other advantages on earth. You have to learn the paraphrases and the shorter catechism; you generally take to drink; your youth, as far as I can find out, is a time of louder war against society, of more outcry and tears and turmoil, than if you had been born, for instance, in England. But somehow life is warmer and closer; the hearth burns more redly; the lights of home shine softer on the rainy street; the very names, endeared in verse and music, cling nearer round our hearts. An Englishman may meet an Englishman to-morrow, upon Chimborazo, and neither of them care; but when the Scotch wine-grower told me of Mons Meg, it was like magic.

"From the dim shieling on the misty island Mountains divide us, and a world of seas; Yet still our hearts are true, our hearts are Highland, And we, in dreams, behold the Hebrides."

And, Highland and Lowland, all our hearts are Scotch.

Only a few days after I had seen M'Eckron, a message reached me in my cottage. It was a Scotchman who had come down a long way from the hills to market. He had heard there was a countryman in Calistoga, and came round to the hotel to see him. We said a few words to each other; we had not much to say--should never have seen each other had we stayed at home, separated alike in space and in society; and then we shook hands, and he went his way again to his ranche among the hills, and that was all.

Another Scotchman there was, a resident, who for the more love of the common country, douce, serious, religious man, drove me all about the valley, and took as much interest in me as if I had been his son: more, perhaps; for the son has faults too keenly felt, while the abstract countryman is perfect--like a whiff of peats.

And there was yet another. Upon him I came suddenly, as he was calmly entering my cottage, his mind quite evidently bent on plunder: a man of about fifty, filthy, ragged, roguish, with a chimney-pot hat and a tail coat, and a pursing of his mouth that might have been envied by an elder of the kirk. He had just such a face as I have seen a dozen times behind the plate.

"Hullo, sir!" I cried. "Where are you going?"

He turned round without a quiver.

"You're a Scotchman, sir?" he said gravely. "So am I; I come from Aberdeen. This is my card," presenting me with a piece of pasteboard which he had raked out of some gutter in the period of the rains. "I was just examining this palm," he continued, indicating the misbegotten plant before our door, "which is the largest spAcimen I have yet observed in Califoarnia."

There were four or five larger within sight. But where was the use of argument? He produced a tape-line, made me help him to measure the tree at the level of the ground, and entered the figures in a large and filthy pocket-book, all with the gravity of Solomon. He then thanked me profusely, remarking that such little services were due between countrymen; shook hands with me, "for add lang syne," as he said; and took himself solemnly away, radiating dirt and humbug as he went.

A month or two after this encounter of mine, there came a Scot to Sacramento--perhaps from Aberdeen. Anyway, there never was any one more Scotch in this wide world. He could sing and dance, and drink, I presume; and he played the pipes with vigour and success. All the Scotch in Sacramento became infatuated with him, and spent their spare time and money, driving him about in an open cab, between drinks, while he blew himself scarlet at the pipes. This is a very sad story. After he had borrowed money from every one, he and his pipes suddenly disappeared from Sacramento, and when I last heard, the police were looking for him.

I cannot say how this story amused me, when I felt myself so thoroughly ripe on both sides to be duped in the same way.

It is at least a curious thing, to conclude, that the races which wander widest, Jews and Scotch, should be the most clannish in the world. But perhaps these two are cause and effect: "For ye were strangers in the land of Egypt."

PART II--WITH THE CHILDREN OF ISRAEL

CHAPTER I.--TO INTRODUCE MR. KELMAR

One thing in this new country very particularly strikes a stranger, and that is the number of antiquities. Already there have been many cycles of population succeeding each other, and passing away and leaving behind them relics. These, standing on into changed times, strike the imagination as forcibly as any pyramid or feudal tower. The towns, like the vineyards, are experimentally founded: they grow great and prosper by passing occasions; and when the lode comes to an end, and the miners move elsewhere, the town remains behind them, like Palmyra in the desert. I suppose there are, in no country in the world, so many deserted towns as here in California.

The whole neighbourhood of Mount Saint Helena, now so quiet and sylvan, was once alive with mining camps and villages. Here there would be two thousand souls under canvas; there one thousand or fifteen hundred ensconced, as if for ever, in a town of comfortable houses. But the luck had failed, the mines petered out; and the army of miners had departed, and left this quarter of the world to the rattlesnakes and deer and grizzlies, and to the slower but steadier advance of husbandry.

It was with an eye on one of these deserted places, Pine Flat, on the Geysers road, that we had come first to Calistoga. There is something singularly enticing in the idea of going, rent-free, into a ready-made house. And to the British merchant, sitting at home at ease, it may appear that, with such a roof over your head and a spring of clear water hard by, the whole problem of the squatter's existence would be solved. Food, however, has yet to be considered, I will go as far as most people on tinned meats; some of the brightest moments of my life were passed over tinned mulli- gatawney in the cabin of a sixteen-ton schooner, storm-stayed in Portree Bay; but after suitable experiments, I pronounce authoritatively that man cannot live by tins alone. Fresh meat must be had on an occasion. It is true that the great Foss, driving by along the Geysers road, wooden-faced, but glorified with legend, might have been induced to bring us meat, but the great Foss could hardly bring us milk. To take a cow would have involved taking a field of grass and a milkmaid; after which it would have been hardly worth while to pause, and we might have added to our colony a flock of sheep and an experienced butcher.

It is really very disheartening how we depend on other people in this life. "Mihi est propositum," as you may see by the motto, "id quod regibus;" and behold it cannot be carried out, unless I find a neighbour rolling in cattle.

Now, my principal adviser in this matter was one whom I will call Kelmar. That was not what he called himself, but as soon as I set eyes on him, I knew it was or ought to be his name; I am sure it will be his name among the angels. Kelmar was the store-keeper, a Russian Jew, good-natured, in a very thriving way of business, and, on equal terms, one of the most serviceable of men. He also had something of the expression of a Scotch country elder, who, by some peculiarity, should chance to be a Hebrew. He had a projecting under lip, with which he continually smiled, or rather smirked. Mrs. Kelmar was a singularly kind woman; and the oldest son had quite a dark and romantic bearing, and might be heard on summer evenings playing sentimental airs on the violin.

I had no idea, at the time I made his acquaintance, what an important person Kelmar was. But the Jew store-keepers of California, profiting at once by the needs and habits of the people, have made themselves in too many cases the tyrants of the rural population. Credit is offered, is pressed on the new customer, and when once he is beyond his depth, the tune changes, and he is from thenceforth a white slave. I believe, even from the little I saw, that Kelmar, if he choose to put on the screw, could send half the settlers packing in a radius of seven or eight miles round Calistoga. These are continually paying him, but are never suffered to get out of debt. He palms dull goods upon them, for they dare not refuse to buy; he goes and dines with them when he is on an outing, and no man is loudlier welcomed; he is their family friend, the director of their business, and, to a degree elsewhere unknown in modern days, their king.

For some reason, Kelmar always shook his head at the mention of Pine Flat, and for some days I thought he disapproved of the whole scheme and was proportionately sad. One fine morning, however, he met me, wreathed in smiles. He had found the very place for me-- Silverado, another old mining town, right up the mountain. Rufe Hanson, the hunter, could take care of us--fine people the Hansons; we should be close to the Toll House, where the Lakeport stage called daily; it was the best place for my health, besides. Rufe had been consumptive, and was now quite a strong man, ain't it? In short, the place and all its accompaniments seemed made for us on purpose.

He took me to his back door, whence, as from every point of Calistoga, Mount Saint Helena could be seen towering in the air. There, in the nick, just where the eastern foothills joined the mountain, and she herself began to rise above the zone of forest-- there was Silverado. The name had already pleased me; the high station pleased me still more. I began to inquire with some eagerness. It was but a little while ago that Silverado was a great place. The mine--a silver mine, of course--had promised great things. There was quite a lively population, with several hotels and boarding-houses; and Kelmar himself had opened a branch store, and done extremely well--"Ain't it?" he said, appealing to his wife. And she said, "Yes; extremely well." Now there was no one living in the town but Rufe the hunter; and once more I heard Rufe's praises by the yard, and this time sung in chorus.

I could not help perceiving at the time that there was something underneath; that no unmixed desire to have us comfortably settled had inspired the Kelmars with this flow of words. But I was impatient to be gone, to be about my kingly project; and when we were offered seats in Kelmar's waggon, I accepted on the spot. The plan of their next Sunday's outing took them, by good fortune, over the border into Lake County. They would carry us so far, drop us at the Toll House, present us to the Hansons, and call for us again on Monday morning early.

CHAPTER II--FIRST IMPRESSIONS OF SILVERADO

We were to leave by six precisely; that was solemnly pledged on both sides; and a messenger came to us the last thing at night, to remind us of the hour. But it was eight before we got clear of Calistoga: Kelmar, Mrs. Kelmar, a friend of theirs whom we named Abramina, her little daughter, my wife, myself, and, stowed away behind us, a cluster of ship's coffee-kettles. These last were highly ornamental in the sheen of their bright tin, but I could invent no reason for their presence. Our carriageful reckoned up, as near as we could get at it, some three hundred years to the six of us. Four of the six, besides, were Hebrews. But I never, in all my life, was conscious of so strong an atmosphere of holiday. No word was spoken but of pleasure; and even when we drove in silence, nods and smiles went round the party like refreshments.

The sun shone out of a cloudless sky. Close at the zenith rode the belated moon, still clearly visible, and, along one margin, even bright. The wind blew a gale from the north; the trees roared; the corn and the deep grass in the valley fled in whitening surges; the dust towered into the air along the road and dispersed like the smoke of battle. It was clear in our teeth from the first, and for all the windings of the road it managed to keep clear in our teeth until the end.

For some two miles we rattled through the valley, skirting the eastern foothills; then we struck off to the right, through haugh- land, and presently, crossing a dry water-course, entered the Toll road, or, to be more local, entered on "the grade." The road mounts the near shoulder of Mount Saint Helena, bound northward into Lake County. In one place it skirts along the edge of a narrow and deep canyon, filled with trees, and I was glad, indeed, not to be driven at this point by the dashing Foss. Kelmar, with his unvarying smile, jogging to the motion of the trap, drove for all the world like a good, plain, country clergyman at home; and I profess I blessed him unawares for his timidity.

Vineyards and deep meadows, islanded and framed with thicket, gave place more and more as we ascended to woods of oak and madrona, dotted with enormous pines. It was these pines, as they shot above the lower wood, that produced that pencilling of single trees I had so often remarked from the valley. Thence, looking up and from however far, each fir stands separate against the sky no bigger than an eyelash; and all together lend a quaint, fringed aspect to the hills. The oak is no baby; even the madrona, upon these spurs of Mount Saint Helena, comes to a fine bulk and ranks with forest trees--but the pines look down upon the rest for underwood. As Mount Saint Helena among her foothills, so these dark giants out- top their fellow-vegetables. Alas! if they had left the redwoods, the pines, in turn, would have been dwarfed. But the redwoods, fallen from their high estate, are serving as family bedsteads, or yet more humbly as field fences, along all Napa Valley.

A rough smack of resin was in the air, and a crystal mountain purity. It came pouring over these green slopes by the oceanful. The woods sang aloud, and gave largely of their healthful breath. Gladness seemed to inhabit these upper zones, and we had left indifference behind us in the valley. "I to the hills lift mine eyes!" There are days in a life when thus to climb out of the lowlands, seems like scaling heaven.

As we continued to ascend, the wind fell upon us with increasing strength. It was a wonder how the two stout horses managed to pull us up that steep incline and still face the athletic opposition of the wind, or how their great eyes were able to endure the dust. Ten minutes after we went by, a tree fell, blocking the road; and even before us leaves were thickly strewn, and boughs had fallen, large enough to make the passage difficult. But now we were hard by the summit. The road crosses the ridge, just in the nick that Kelmar showed me from below, and then, without pause, plunges down a deep, thickly wooded glen on the farther side. At the highest point a trail strikes up the main hill to the leftward; and that leads to Silverado. A hundred yards beyond, and in a kind of elbow of the glen, stands the Toll House Hotel. We came up the one side, were caught upon the summit by the whole weight of the wind as it poured over into Napa Valley, and a minute after had drawn up in shelter, but all buffetted and breathless, at the Toll House door.

A water-tank, and stables, and a gray house of two stories, with gable ends and a verandah, are jammed hard against the hillside, just where a stream has cut for itself a narrow canyon, filled with pines. The pines go right up overhead; a little more and the stream might have played, like a fire-hose, on the Toll House roof. In front the ground drops as sharply as it rises behind. There is just room for the road and a sort of promontory of croquet ground, and then you can lean over the edge and look deep below you through the wood. I said croquet GROUND, not GREEN; for the surface was of brown, beaten earth. The toll-bar itself was the only other note of originality: a long beam, turning on a post, and kept slightly horizontal by a counterweight of stones. Regularly about sundown this rude barrier was swung, like a derrick, across the road and made fast, I think, to a tree upon the farther side.

On our arrival there followed a gay scene in the bar. I was presented to Mr. Corwin, the landlord; to Mr. Jennings, the engineer, who lives there for his health; to Mr. Hoddy, a most pleasant little gentleman, once a member of the Ohio legislature, again the editor of a local paper, and now, with undiminished dignity, keeping the Toll House bar. I had a number of drinks and cigars bestowed on me, and enjoyed a famous opportunity of seeing Kelmar in his glory, friendly, radiant, smiling, steadily edging one of the ship's kettles on the reluctant Corwin.

Corwin, plainly aghast, resisted gallantly, and for that bout victory crowned his arms.

At last we set forth for Silverado on foot. Kelmar and his jolly Jew girls were full of the sentiment of Sunday outings, breathed geniality and vagueness, and suffered a little vile boy from the hotel to lead them here and there about the woods. For three people all so old, so bulky in body, and belonging to a race so venerable, they could not but surprise us by their extreme and almost imbecile youthfulness of spirit. They were only going to stay ten minutes at the Toll House; had they not twenty long miles of road before them on the other side? Stay to dinner? Not they! Put up the horses? Never. Let us attach them to the verandah by a wisp of straw rope, such as would not have held a person's hat on that blustering day. And with all these protestations of hurry, they proved irresponsible like children. Kelmar himself, shrewd old Russian Jew, with a smirk that seemed just to have concluded a bargain to its satisfaction, intrusted himself and us devoutly to that boy. Yet the boy was patently fallacious; and for that matter a most unsympathetic urchin, raised apparently on gingerbread. He was bent on his own pleasure, nothing else; and Kelmar followed him to his ruin, with the same shrewd smirk. If the boy said there was "a hole there in the hill"--a hole, pure and simple, neither more nor less--Kelmar and his Jew girls would follow him a hundred yards to look complacently down that hole. For two hours we looked for houses; and for two hours they followed us, smelling trees, picking flowers, foisting false botany on the unwary. Had we taken five, with that vile lad to head them off on idle divagations, for five they would have smiled and stumbled through the woods.

However, we came forth at length, and as by accident, upon a lawn, sparse planted like an orchard, but with forest instead of fruit trees. That was the site of Silverado mining town. A piece of ground was levelled up, where Kelmar's store had been; and facing that we saw Rufe Hanson's house, still bearing on its front the legend Silverado Hotel. Not another sign of habitation. Silverado town had all been carted from the scene; one of the houses was now the school-house far down the road; one was gone here, one there, but all were gone away.

It was now a sylvan solitude, and the silence was unbroken but by the great, vague voice of the wind. Some days before our visit, a grizzly bear had been sporting round the Hansons' chicken-house.

Mrs. Hanson was at home alone, we found. Rufe had been out after a "bar," had risen late, and was now gone, it did not clearly appear whither. Perhaps he had had wind of Kelmar's coming, and was now ensconced among the underwood, or watching us from the shoulder of the mountain. We, hearing there were no houses to be had, were for immediately giving up all hopes of Silverado. But this, somehow, was not to Kelmar's fancy. He first proposed that we should "camp someveres around, ain't it?" waving his hand cheerily as though to weave a spell; and when that was firmly rejected, he decided that we must take up house with the Hansons. Mrs. Hanson had been, from the first, flustered, subdued, and a little pale; but from this proposition she recoiled with haggard indignation. So did we, who would have preferred, in a manner of speaking, death. But Kelmar was not to be put by. He edged Mrs. Hanson into a corner, where for a long time he threatened her with his forefinger, like a character in Dickens; and the poor woman, driven to her entrenchments, at last remembered with a shriek that there were still some houses at the tunnel.

Thither we went; the Jews, who should already have been miles into Lake County, still cheerily accompanying us. For about a furlong we followed a good road alone, the hillside through the forest, until suddenly that road widened out and came abruptly to an end. A canyon, woody below, red, rocky, and naked overhead, was here walled across by a dump of rolling stones, dangerously steep, and from twenty to thirty feet in height. A rusty iron chute on wooden legs came flying, like a monstrous gargoyle, across the parapet. It was down this that they poured the precious ore; and below here the carts stood to wait their lading, and carry it mill-ward down the mountain.

The whole canyon was so entirely blocked, as if by some rude guerilla fortification, that we could only mount by lengths of wooden ladder, fixed in the hillside. These led us round the farther corner of the dump; and when they were at an end, we still persevered over loose rubble and wading deep in poison oak, till we struck a triangular platform, filling up the whole glen, and shut in on either hand by bold projections of the mountain. Only in front the place was open like the proscenium of a theatre, and we looked forth into a great realm of air, and down upon treetops and hilltops, and far and near on wild and varied country. The place still stood as on the day it was deserted: a line of iron rails with a bifurcation; a truck in working order; a world of lumber, old wood, old iron; a blacksmith's forge on one side, half buried in the leaves of dwarf madronas; and on the other, an old brown wooden house.

Fanny and I dashed at the house. It consisted of three rooms, and was so plastered against the hill, that one room was right atop of another, that the upper floor was more than twice as large as the lower, and that all three apartments must be entered from a different side and level. Not a window-sash remained.

The door of the lower room was smashed, and one panel hung in splinters. We entered that, and found a fair amount of rubbish: sand and gravel that had been sifted in there by the mountain winds; straw, sticks, and stones; a table, a barrel; a plate-rack on the wall; two home-made bootjacks, signs of miners and their boots; and a pair of papers pinned on the boarding, headed respectively "Funnel No. 1," and "Funnel No. 2," but with the tails torn away. The window, sashless of course, was choked with the green and sweetly smelling foliage of a bay; and through a chink in the floor, a spray of poison oak had shot up and was handsomely prospering in the interior. It was my first care to cut away that poison oak, Fanny standing by at a respectful distance. That was our first improvement by which we took possession.

The room immediately above could only be entered by a plank propped against the threshold, along which the intruder must foot it gingerly, clutching for support to sprays of poison oak, the proper product of the country. Herein was, on either hand, a triple tier of beds, where miners had once lain; and the other gable was pierced by a sashless window and a doorless doorway opening on the air of heaven, five feet above the ground. As for the third room, which entered squarely from the ground level, but higher up the hill and farther up the canyon, it contained only rubbish and the uprights for another triple tier of beds.

The whole building was overhung by a bold, lion-like, red rock. Poison oak, sweet bay trees, calcanthus, brush, and chaparral, grew freely but sparsely all about it. In front, in the strong sunshine, the platform lay overstrewn with busy litter, as though the labours of the mine might begin again to-morrow in the morning.

Following back into the canyon, among the mass of rotting plant and through the flowering bushes, we came to a great crazy staging, with a wry windless on the top; and clambering up, we could look into an open shaft, leading edgeways down into the bowels of the mountain, trickling with water, and lit by some stray sun-gleams, whence I know not. In that quiet place the still, far-away tinkle of the water-drops was loudly audible. Close by, another shaft led edgeways up into the superincumbent shoulder of the hill. It lay partly open; and sixty or a hundred feet above our head, we could see the strata propped apart by solid wooden wedges, and a pine, half undermined, precariously nodding on the verge. Here also a rugged, horizontal tunnel ran straight into the unsunned bowels of the rock. This secure angle in the mountain's flank was, even on this wild day, as still as my lady's chamber. But in the tunnel a cold, wet draught tempestuously blew. Nor have I ever known that place otherwise than cold and windy.

Such was our fist prospect of Juan Silverado. I own I had looked for something different: a clique of neighbourly houses on a village green, we shall say, all empty to be sure, but swept and varnished; a trout stream brawling by; great elms or chestnuts, humming with bees and nested in by song-birds; and the mountains standing round about, as at Jerusalem. Here, mountain and house and the old tools of industry were all alike rusty and downfalling. The hill was here wedged up, and there poured forth its bowels in a spout of broken mineral; man with his picks and powder, and nature with her own great blasting tools of sun and rain, labouring together at the ruin of that proud mountain. The view up the canyon was a glimpse of devastation; dry red minerals sliding together, here and there a crag, here and there dwarf thicket clinging in the general glissade, and over all a broken outline trenching on the blue of heaven. Downwards indeed, from our rock eyrie, we behold the greener side of nature; and the bearing of the pines and the sweet smell of bays and nutmegs commanded themselves gratefully to our senses. One way and another, now the die was cast. Silverado be it!

After we had got back to the Toll House, the Jews were not long of striking forward. But I observed that one of the Hanson lads came down, before their departure, and returned with a ship's kettle. Happy Hansons! Nor was it until after Kelmar was gone, if I remember rightly, that Rufe put in an appearance to arrange the details of our installation.

The latter part of the day, Fanny and I sat in the verandah of the Toll House, utterly stunned by the uproar of the wind among the trees on the other side of the valley. Sometimes, we would have it it was like a sea, but it was not various enough for that; and again, we thought it like the roar of a cataract, but it was too changeful for the cataract; and then we would decide, speaking in sleepy voices, that it could be compared with nothing but itself. My mind was entirely preoccupied by the noise. I hearkened to it by the hour, gapingly hearkened, and let my cigarette go out. Sometimes the wind would make a sally nearer hand, and send a shrill, whistling crash among the foliage on our side of the glen; and sometimes a back-draught would strike into the elbow where we sat, and cast the gravel and torn leaves into our faces. But for the most part, this great, streaming gale passed unweariedly by us into Napa Valley, not two hundred yards away, visible by the tossing boughs, stunningly audible, and yet not moving a hair upon our heads. So it blew all night long while I was writing up my journal, and after we were in bed, under a cloudless, starset heaven; and so it was blowing still next morning when we rose.

It was a laughable thought to us, what had become of our cheerful, wandering Hebrews. We could not suppose they had reached a destination. The meanest boy could lead them miles out of their way to see a gopher-hole. Boys, we felt to be their special danger; none others were of that exact pitch of cheerful irrelevancy to exercise a kindred sway upon their minds: but before the attractions of a boy their most settled resolutions would be war. We thought we could follow in fancy these three aged Hebrew truants wandering in and out on hilltop and in thicket, a demon boy trotting far ahead, their will-o'-the-wisp conductor; and at last about midnight, the wind still roaring in the darkness, we had a vision of all three on their knees upon a mountain-top around a glow-worm.

CHAPTER III. THE RETURN

Next morning we were up by half-past five, according to agreement, and it was ten by the clock before our Jew boys returned to pick us up. Kelmar, Mrs. Kelmar, and Abramina, all smiling from ear to ear, and full of tales of the hospitality they had found on the other side. It had not gone un-rewarded; for I observed with interest that the ship's kettles, all but one, had been "placed." Three Lake County families, at least, endowed for life with a ship's kettle. Come, this was no misspent Sunday. The absence of the kettles told its own story: our Jews said nothing about them; but, on the other hand, they said many kind and comely things about the people they had met. The two women, in particular, had been charmed out of themselves by the sight of a young girl surrounded by her admirers; all evening, it appeared, they had been triumphing together in the girl's innocent successes, and to this natural and unselfish joy they gave expression in language that was beautiful by its simplicity and truth.

Take them for all in all, few people have done my heart more good; they seemed so thoroughly entitled to happiness, and to enjoy it in so large a measure and so free from after-thought; almost they persuaded me to be a Jew. There was, indeed, a chink of money in their talk. They particularly commanded people who were well to do. "HE don't care--ain't it?" was their highest word of commendation to an individual fate; and here I seem to grasp the root of their philosophy--it was to be free from care, to be free to make these Sunday wanderings, that they so eagerly pursued after wealth; and all this carefulness was to be careless. The fine, good humour of all three seemed to declare they had attained their end. Yet there was the other side to it; and the recipients of kettles perhaps cared greatly.

No sooner had they returned, than the scene of yesterday began again. The horses were not even tied with a straw rope this time-- it was not worth while; and

Kelmar disappeared into the bar, leaving them under a tree on the other side of the road. I had to devote myself. I stood under the shadow of that tree for, I suppose, hard upon an hour, and had not the heart to be angry. Once some one remembered me, and brought me out half a tumblerful of the playful, innocuous American cocktail. I drank it, and lo! veins of living fire ran down my leg; and then a focus of conflagration remained seated in my stomach, not unpleasantly, for quarter of an hour. I love these sweet, fiery pangs, but I will not court them. The bulk of the time I spent in repeating as much French poetry as I could remember to the horses, who seemed to enjoy it hugely. And now it went -

"O ma vieille Font-georges Ou volent les rouges-gorges:"

and again, to a more trampling measure -

"Et tout tremble, Irun, Coimbre, Sautander, Almodovar, Sitot qu'on entend le timbre Des cymbales do Bivar."

The redbreasts and the brooks of Europe, in that dry and songless land; brave old names and wars, strong cities, cymbals, and bright armour, in that nook of the mountain, sacred only to the Indian and the bear! This is still the strangest thing in all man's travelling, that he should carry about with him incongruous memories. There is no foreign land; it is the traveller only that is foreign, and now and again, by a flash of recollection, lights up the contrasts of the earth.

But while I was thus wandering in my fancy, great feats had been transacted in the bar. Corwin the bold had fallen, Kelmar was again crowned with laurels, and the last of the ship's kettles had changed hands. If I had ever doubted the purity of Kelmar's motives, if I had ever suspected him of a single eye to business in his eternal dallyings, now at least, when the last kettle was disposed of, my suspicions must have been allayed. I dare not guess how much more time was wasted; nor how often we drove off, merely to drive back again and renew interrupted conversations about nothing, before the Toll House was fairly left behind. Alas! and not a mile down the grade there stands a ranche in a sunny vineyard, and here we must all dismount again and enter.

Only the old lady was at home, Mrs. Guele, a brown old Swiss dame, the picture of honesty; and with her we drank a bottle of wine and had an age-long conversation, which would have been highly delightful if Fanny and I had not been faint with hunger. The ladies each narrated the story of her marriage, our two Hebrews with the prettiest combination of sentiment and financial bathos. Abramina, specially, endeared herself with every word. She was as simple, natural, and engaging as a kid that should have been brought up to the business of a money-changer. One touch was so resplendently Hebraic that I cannot pass it over. When her "old man" wrote home for her from America, her old man's family would not intrust her with the money for the passage, till she had bound herself by an oath--on her knees, I think she said--not to employ it otherwise.

This had tickled Abramina hugely, but I think it tickled me fully more.

Mrs. Guele told of her home-sickness up here in the long winters; of her honest, country-woman troubles and alarms upon the journey; how in the bank at Frankfort she had feared lest the banker, after having taken her cheque, should deny all knowledge of it--a fear I have myself every time I go to a bank; and how crossing the Luneburger Heath, an old lady, witnessing her trouble and finding whither she was bound, had given her "the blessing of a person eighty years old, which would be sure to bring her safely to the States. And the first thing I did," added Mrs. Guele, "was to fall downstairs."

At length we got out of the house, and some of us into the trap, when--judgment of Heaven!--here came Mr. Guele from his vineyard. So another quarter of an hour went by; till at length, at our earnest pleading, we set forth again in earnest, Fanny and I white- faced and silent, but the Jews still smiling. The heart fails me. There was yet another stoppage! And we drove at last into Calistoga past two in the afternoon, Fanny and I having breakfasted at six in the morning, eight mortal hours before. We were a pallid couple; but still the Jews were smiling.

So ended our excursion with the village usurers; and, now that it was done, we had no more idea of the nature of the business, nor of the part we had been playing in it, than the child unborn. That all the people we had met were the slaves of Kelmar, though in various degrees of servitude; that we ourselves had been sent up the mountain in the interests of none but Kelmar; that the money we laid out, dollar by dollar, cent by cent, and through the hands of various intermediaries, should all hop ultimately into Kelmar's till;--these were facts that we only grew to recognize in the course of time and by the accumulation of evidence. At length all doubt was quieted, when one of the kettle-holders confessed. Stopping his trap in the moonlight, a little way out of Calistoga, he told me, in so many words, that he dare not show face therewith an empty pocket. "You see, I don't mind if it was only five dollars, Mr. Stevens," he said, "but I must give Mr. Kelmar SOMETHING."

Even now, when the whole tyranny is plain to me, I cannot find it in my heart to be as angry as perhaps I should be with the Hebrew tyrant. The whole game of business is beggar my neighbour; and though perhaps that game looks uglier when played at such close quarters and on so small a scale, it is none the more intrinsically inhumane for that. The village usurer is not so sad a feature of humanity and human progress as the millionaire manufacturer, fattening on the toil and loss of thousands, and yet declaiming from the platform against the greed and dishonesty of landlords. If it were fair for Cobden to buy up land from owners whom he thought unconscious of its proper value, it was fair enough for my Russian Jew to give credit to his farmers. Kelmar, if he was unconscious of the beam in his own eye, was at least silent in the matter of his brother's mote.

THE ACT OF SQUATTING

There were four of us squatters--myself and my wife, the King and Queen of Silverado; Sam, the Crown Prince; and Chuchu, the Grand Duke. Chuchu, a setter crossed with spaniel, was the most unsuited for a rough life. He had been nurtured tenderly in the society of ladies; his heart was large and soft; he regarded the sofa-cushion as a bed-rook necessary of existence. Though about the size of a sheep, he loved to sit in ladies' laps; he never said a bad word in all his blameless days; and if he had seen a flute, I am sure he could have played upon it by nature. It may seem hard to say it of a dog, but Chuchu was a tame cat.

The king and queen, the grand duke, and a basket of cold provender for immediate use, set forth from Calistoga in a double buggy; the crown prince, on horseback, led the way like an outrider. Bags and boxes and a second-hand stove were to follow close upon our heels by Hanson's team.

It was a beautiful still day; the sky was one field of azure. Not a leaf moved, not a speck appeared in heaven. Only from the summit of the mountain one little snowy wisp of cloud after another kept detaching itself, like smoke from a volcano, and blowing southward in some high stream of air: Mount Saint Helena still at her interminable task, making the weather, like a Lapland witch.

By noon we had come in sight of the mill: a great brown building, half-way up the hill, big as a factory, two stories high, and with tanks and ladders along the roof; which, as a pendicle of Silverado mine, we held to be an outlying province of our own. Thither, then, we went, crossing the valley by a grassy trail; and there lunched out of the basket, sitting in a kind of portico, and wondering, while we ate, at this great bulk of useless building. Through a chink we could look far down into the interior, and see sunbeams floating in the dust and striking on tier after tier of silent, rusty machinery. It cost six thousand dollars, twelve hundred English sovereigns; and now, here it stands deserted, like the temple of a forgotten religion, the busy millers toiling somewhere else. All the time we were there, mill and mill town showed no sign of life; that part of the mountain-side, which is very open and green, was tenanted by no living creature but ourselves and the insects; and nothing stirred but the cloud manufactory upon the mountain summit. It was odd to compare this with the former days, when the engine was in fall blast, the mill palpitating to its strokes, and the carts came rattling down from Silverado, charged with ore.

By two we had been landed at the mine, the buggy was gone again, and we were left to our own reflections and the basket of cold provender, until Hanson should arrive. Hot as it was by the sun, there was something chill in such a home-coming, in that world of wreck and rust, splinter and rolling gravel, where for so many years no fire had smoked.

Silverado platform filled the whole width of the canyon. Above, as I have said, this was a wild, red, stony gully in the mountains; but below it was a wooded dingle. And through this, I was told, there had gone a path between the mine and the Toll House--our natural north-west passage to civilization. I found and fol-lowed it, clearing my way as I went through fallen branches and dead trees. It went straight down that steep canyon, till it brought you out abruptly over the roofs of the hotel. There was nowhere any break in the descent. It almost seemed as if, were you to drop a stone down the old iron chute at our platform, it would never rest until it hopped upon the Toll House shingles. Signs were not wanting of the ancient greatness of Silverado. The footpath was well marked, and had been well trodden in the old clays by thirsty miners. And far down, buried in foliage, deep out of sight of Silverado, I came on a last outpost of the mine--a mound of gravel, some wreck of wooden aqueduct, and the mouth of a tunnel, like a treasure grotto in a fairy story. A stream of water, fed by the invisible leakage from our shaft, and dyed red with cinnabar or iron, ran trippingly forth out of the bowels of the cave; and, looking far under the arch, I could see something like an iron lantern fastened on the rocky wall. It was a promising spot for the imagination. No boy could have left it unexplored.

The stream thenceforward stole along the bottom of the dingle, and made, for that dry land, a pleasant warbling in the leaves. Once, I suppose, it ran splashing down the whole length of the canyon, but now its head waters had been tapped by the shaft at Silverado, and for a great part of its course it wandered sunless among the joints of the mountain. No wonder that it should better its pace when it sees, far before it, daylight whitening in the arch, or that it should come trotting forth into the sunlight with a song.

The two stages had gone by when I got down, and the Toll House stood, dozing in sun and dust and silence, like a place enchanted. My mission was after hay for bedding, and that I was readily promised. But when I mentioned that we were waiting for Rufe, the people shook their heads. Rufe was not a regular man any way, it seemed; and if he got playing poker--Well, poker was too many for Rufe. I had not yet heard them bracketted together; but it seemed a natural conjunction, and commended itself swiftly to my fears; and as soon as I returned to Silverado and had told my story, we practically gave Hanson up, and set ourselves to do what we could find do-able in our desert-island state.

The lower room had been the assayer's office. The floor was thick with debris--part human, from the former occupants; part natural, sifted in by mountain winds. In a sea of red dust there swam or floated sticks, boards, hay, straw, stones, and paper; ancient newspapers, above all--for the newspaper, especially when torn, soon becomes an antiquity--and bills of the Silverado boarding- house, some dated Silverado, some Calistoga Mine. Here is one, verbatim; and if any one can calculate the scale of charges, he has my envious admiration.

Where is John Stanley mining now? Where is S. Chapman, within whose hospitable walls we were to lodge? The date was but five years old, but in that time the world had changed for Silverado; like Palmyra in the desert, it had outlived its people and its purpose; we camped, like Layard, amid ruins, and these names spoke to us of prehistoric time. A boot-jack, a pair of boots, a dog- hutch, and these bills of Mr. Chapman's were the only speaking relics that we disinterred from all that vast Silverado rubbish- heap; but what would I not have given to unearth a letter, a pocket-book, a diary, only a ledger, or a roll of names, to take me back, in a more personal manner, to the past? It pleases me, besides, to fancy that Stanley or Chapman, or one of their companions, may light upon this chronicle, and be struck by the name, and read some news of their anterior home, coming, as it were, out of a subsequent epoch of history in that quarter of the world.

As we were tumbling the mingled rubbish on the floor, kicking it with our feet, and groping for these written evidences of the past, Sam, with a somewhat whitened face, produced a paper bag. "What's this?" said he. It contained a granulated powder, something the colour of Gregory's Mixture, but rosier; and as there were several of the bags, and each more or less broken, the powder was spread widely on the floor. Had any of us ever seen giant powder? No, nobody had; and instantly there grew up in my mind a shadowy belief, verging with every moment nearer to certitude, that I had somewhere heard somebody describe it as just such a powder as the one around us. I have learnt since that it is a substance not unlike tallow, and is made up in rolls for all the world like tallow candles.

Fanny, to add to our happiness, told us a story of a gentleman who had camped one night, like ourselves, by a deserted mine. He was a handy, thrifty fellow, and looked right and left for plunder, but all he could lay his hands on was a can of oil. After dark he had to see to the horses with a lantern; and not to miss an opportunity, filled up his lamp from the oil can. Thus equipped, he set forth into the forest. A little while after, his friends heard a loud explosion; the mountain echoes bellowed, and then all was still. On examination, the can proved to contain oil, with the trifling addition of nitro-glycerine; but no research disclosed a trace of either man or lantern.

It was a pretty sight, after this anecdote, to see us sweeping out the giant powder. It seemed never to be far enough away. And, after all, it was only some rock pounded for assay.

So much for the lower room. We scraped some of the rougher dirt off the floor, and left it. That was our sitting-room and kitchen, though there was nothing to sit upon but the table, and no provision for a fire except a hole in the roof of the room above, which had once contained the chimney of a stove.

To that upper room we now proceeded. There were the eighteen bunks in a double tier, nine on either hand, where from eighteen to thirty-six miners had once snored together all night long, John Stanley, perhaps, snoring loudest. There was the roof, with a hole in it through which the sun now shot an arrow. There was the floor, in much the same state as the one below, though, perhaps, there was more hay, and certainly there was the added ingredient of broken glass, the man who stole the window-frames having apparently made a miscarriage with this one. Without a broom, without hay or bedding, we could but look about us with a beginning of despair. The one bright arrow of day, in that gaunt and shattered barrack, made the rest look dirtier and darker, and the sight drove us at last into the open.

Here, also, the handiwork of man lay ruined: but the plants were all alive and thriving; the view below was fresh with the colours of nature; and we had exchanged a dim, human garret for a corner, even although it were untidy, of the blue hall of heaven. Not a bird, not a beast, not a reptile. There was no noise in that part of the world, save when we passed beside the staging, and heard the water musically falling in the shaft.

We wandered to and fro. We searched among that drift of lumber- wood and iron, nails and rails, and sleepers and the wheels of tracks. We gazed up the cleft into the bosom of the mountain. We sat by the margin of the dump and saw, far below us, the green treetops standing still in the clear air. Beautiful perfumes, breaths of bay, resin, and nutmeg, came to us more often and grew sweeter and sharper as the afternoon declined. But still there was no word of Hanson.

I set to with pick and shovel, and deepened the pool behind the shaft, till we were sure of sufficient water for the morning; and by the time I had finished, the sun had begun to go down behind the mountain shoulder, the platform was plunged in quiet shadow, and a chill descended from the sky. Night began early in our cleft. Before us, over the margin of the dump, we could see the sun still striking aslant into the wooded nick below, and on the battlemented, pine-bescattered ridges on the farther side.

There was no stove, of course, and no hearth in our lodging, so we betook ourselves to the blacksmith's forge across the platform. If the platform be taken as a stage, and the out-curving margin of the dump to represent the line of the foot-lights, then our house would be the first wing on the actor's left, and this black-smith's forge, although no match for it in size, the foremost on the right. It was a low, brown cottage, planted close against the hill, and overhung by the foliage and peeling boughs of a madrona thicket. Within it was full of dead leaves and moun-tain dust, and rubbish from the mine. But we soon had a good fire brightly blazing, and sat close about it on impromptu seats. Chuchu, the slave of sofa- cushions, whimpered for a softer bed; but the rest of us were greatly revived and comforted by that good creature-fire, which gives us warmth and light and companionable sounds, and colours up the emptiest building with better than frescoes. For a while it was even pleasant in the forge, with the blaze in the midst, and a look over our shoulders on the woods and mountains where the day was dying like a dolphin.

It was between seven and eight before Hanson arrived, with a waggonful of our effects and two of his wife's relatives to lend him a hand. The elder showed sur-prising strength. He would pick up a huge packing-case, full of books of all things, swing it on his shoulder, and away up the two crazy ladders and the breakneck spout of rolling mineral, familiarly termed a path, that led from the cart-track to our house. Even for a man unburthened, the ascent was toilsome and precarious; but Irvine sealed it with a light foot, carrying box after box, as the hero whisks the stage child up the practicable footway beside the waterfall of the fifth act. With so strong a helper, the business was speedily transacted. Soon the assayer's office was thronged with our belongings, piled higgledy-piggledy, and upside down, about the floor. There were our boxes, indeed, but my wife had left her keys in Calistoga. There was the stove, but, alas! our carriers had forgot the chimney, and lost one of the plates along the road. The Silverado problem was scarce solved.

Rufe himself was grave and good-natured over his share of blame; he even, if I remember right, expressed regret. But his crew, to my astonishment and anger, grinned from ear to ear, and laughed aloud at our distress. They thought it "real funny" about the stove-pipe they had forgotten; "real funny" that they should have lost a plate. As for hay, the whole party refused to bring us any till they should have supped. See how late they were! Never had there been such a job as coming up that grade! Nor often, I suspect, such a game of poker as that before they started. But about nine, as a particular favour, we should have some hay.

So they took their departure, leaving me still staring, and we resigned our-selves to wait for their return. The fire in the forge had been suffered to go out, and we were one and all too weary to kindle another. We dined, or, not to take that word in vain, we ate after a fashion, in the nightmare disorder of the assayer's office, perched among boxes. A single candle lighted us. It could scarce be called a housewarming; for there was, of course, no fire, and with the two open doors and the open window gaping on the night, like breaches in a fortress, it began to grow rapidly chill. Talk ceased; nobody moved but the unhappy Chuchu, still in quest of sofa-cushions, who tumbled complainingly among the trunks. It required a certain happiness of disposition to look forward hopefully, from so dismal a beginning, across the brief hours of night, to the warm shining of to-morrow's sun.

But the hay arrived at last, and we turned, with our last spark of courage, to the bedroom. We had improved the entrance, but it was still a kind of rope-walking; and it would have been droll to see us mounting, one after another, by candle-light, under the open stars.

The western door--that which looked up the canyon, and through which we entered by our bridge of flying plank--was still entire, a handsome, panelled door, the most finished piece of carpentry in Silverado. And the two lowest bunks next to this we roughly filled with hay for that night's use. Through the opposite, or east-ern- looking gable, with its open door and window, a faint, disused starshine came into the room like mist; and when we were once in bed, we lay, awaiting sleep, in a haunted, incomplete obscurity. At first the silence of the night was utter. Then a high wind began in the distance among the tree-tops, and for hours continued to grow higher. It seemed to me much such a wind as we had found on our visit; yet here in our open chamber we were fanned only by gentle and refreshing draughts, so deep was the canyon, so close our house was planted under the overhanging rock.

THE HUNTER'S FAMILY

There is quite a large race or class of people in America, for whom we scarcely seem to have a parallel in England. Of pure white blood, they are unknown or unrecognizable in towns; inhabit the fringe of settlements and the deep, quiet places of the country; rebellious to all labour, and pettily thievish, like the English gipsies; rustically ignorant, but with a touch of wood-lore and the dexterity of the savage. Whence they came is a moot point. At the time of the war, they poured north in crowds to escape the conscription; lived during summer on fruits, wild animals, and petty theft; and at the approach of winter, when these supplies failed, built great fires in the forest, and there died stoically by starvation. They are widely scattered, however, and easily recognized. Loutish, but not ill-looking, they will sit all day, swinging their legs on a field fence, the mind seemingly as devoid of all reflection as a Suffolk peasant's, careless of politics, for the most part incapable of reading, but with a rebellious vanity and a strong sense of independence. Hunting is their most congenial business, or, if the occasion offers, a little amateur detection. In tracking a criminal, following a particular horse along a beaten highway, and drawing inductions from a hair or a footprint, one of those somnolent, grinning Hodges will suddenly display activity of body and finesse of mind. By their names ye may know them, the women figuring as Loveina, Larsenia, Serena, Leanna, Orreana; the men answering to Alvin, Alva, or Orion, pronounced Orrion, with the accent on the first. Whether they are indeed a race, or whether this is the form of degeneracy common to all back-woodsmen, they are at least known by a generic byword, as Poor Whites or Low-downers.

I will not say that the Hanson family was Poor White, because the name savours of offence; but I may go as far as this--they were, in many points, not unsimilar to the people usually so-cared. Rufe himself combined two of the qualifications, for he was both a hunter and an amateur detective. It was he who pursued Russel and Dollar, the robbers of the Lake Port stage, and captured them the very morning after the exploit, while they were still sleeping in a hayfield. Russel, a drunken Scotch carpenter, was even an acquaintance of his own, and he expressed much grave commiseration for his fate. In all that he said and did, Rufe was grave. I never saw him hurried. When he spoke, he took out his pipe with ceremonial deliberation, looked east and west, and then, in quiet tones and few words, stated his business or told his story. His gait was to match; it would never have surprised you if, at any step, he had turned round and walked away again, so warily and slowly, and with so much seeming hesitation did he go about. He lay long in bed in the morning--rarely indeed, rose before noon; he loved all games, from poker to clerical croquet; and in the Toll House croquet ground I have seen him toiling at the latter with the devotion of a curate. He took an interest in education, was an active member of the local school-board, and when I was there, he had recently lost the schoolhouse key. His waggon was broken, but it never seemed to occur to him to mend it. Like all truly idle people, he had an artistic eye. He chose the print stuff for his wife's dresses, and counselled her in the making of a patchwork quilt, always, as she thought, wrongly, but to the more educated eye, always with bizarre and admirable taste--the taste of an Indian. With all this, he was a perfect, unoffending gentleman in word and act. Take his clay pipe from him, and he was fit for any society but that of fools. Quiet as he was, there burned a deep, permanent excitement in his dark blue eyes; and when this grave man smiled, it was like sunshine in a shady place.

Mrs. Hanson (nee, if you please, Lovelands) was more commonplace than her lord. She was a comely woman, too, plump, fair-coloured, with wonderful white teeth; and in her print dresses (chosen by Rufe) and with a large sun-bonnet shading her valued complexion, made, I assure you, a very agreeable figure. But she was on the surface, what there was of her, out-spoken and loud-spoken. Her noisy laughter had none of the charm of one of Hanson's rare, slow- spreading smiles; there was no reticence, no mystery, no manner about the woman: she was a first-class dairymaid, but her husband was an unknown quantity between the savage and the nobleman. She was often in and out with us, merry, and healthy, and fair; he came far seldomer--only, indeed, when there was business, or now and again, to pay a visit of ceremony, brushed up for the occasion, with his wife on his arm, and a clean clay pipe in his teeth. These visits, in our forest state, had quite the air of an event, and turned our red canyon into a salon.

Such was the pair who ruled in the old Silverado Hotel, among the windy trees, on the mountain shoulder overlooking the whole length of Napa Valley, as the man aloft looks down on the ship's deck. There they kept house, with sundry horses and fowls, and a family of sons, Daniel Webster, and I think George Washington, among the number. Nor did they want visitors. An old gentleman, of singular stolidity, and called Breedlove--I think he had crossed the plains in the same caravan with Rufe--housed with them for awhile during our stay; and they had besides a permanent lodger, in the form of Mrs. Hanson's brother, Irvine Lovelands. I spell Irvine by guess; for I could get no information on the subject, just as I could never find out, in spite of many inquiries, whether or not Rufe was a contraction for Rufus. They were all cheerfully at sea about their names in that generation. And this is surely the more notable where the names are all so strange, and even the family names appear to have been coined. At one time, at least, the ancestors of all these Alvins and Alvas, Loveinas, Lovelands, and Breedloves, must have taken serious council and found a certain poetry in these denominations; that must have been, then, their form of literature. But still times change; and their next descendants, the George Washingtons and Daniel Websters, will at least be clear upon the point. And anyway, and however his name should be spelt, this Irvine Lovelands was the most unmitigated Caliban I ever knew.

Our very first morning at Silverado, when we were full of business, patching up doors and windows, making beds and seats, and getting our rough lodging into shape, Irvine and his sister made their appearance together, she for neighbourliness and general curiosity; he, because he was working for me, to my sorrow, cutting firewood at I forget how much a day. The way that he set about cutting wood was characteristic. We were at that moment patching up and unpacking in the kitchen. Down he sat on one side, and down sat his sister on the other. Both were chewing pine-tree gum, and he, to my annoyance, accompanied that simple pleasure with profuse expectoration. She rattled away, talking up hill and down dale, laughing, tossing her head, showing her brilliant teeth. He looked on in silence, now spitting heavily on the floor, now putting his head back and uttering a loud, discordant, joyless laugh. He had a tangle of shock hair, the colour of wool; his mouth was a grin; although as strong as a horse, he looked neither heavy nor yet adroit, only leggy, coltish, and in the road. But it was plain he was in high spirits, thoroughly enjoying his visit; and he laughed frankly whenever we failed to accomplish what we were about. This was scarcely helpful: it was even, to amateur carpenters, embarrassing;

but it lasted until we knocked off work and began to get dinner. Then Mrs. Hanson remembered she should have been gone an hour ago; and the pair retired, and the lady's laughter died away among the nutmegs down the path. That was Irvine's first day's work in my employment--the devil take him!

The next morning he returned and, as he was this time alone, he bestowed his conversation upon us with great liberality. He prided himself on his intelligence; asked us if we knew the school ma'am. HE didn't think much of her, anyway. He had tried her, he had. He had put a question to her. If a tree a hundred feet high were to fall a foot a day, how long would it take to fall right down? She had not been able to solve the problem. "She don't know nothing," he opined. He told us how a friend of his kept a school with a revolver, and chuckled mightily over that; his friend could teach school, he could. All the time he kept chewing gum and spitting. He would stand a while looking down; and then he would toss back his shock of hair, and laugh hoarsely, and spit, and bring forward a new subject. A man, he told us, who bore a grudge against him, had poisoned his dog. "That was a low thing for a man to do now, wasn't it? It wasn't like a man, that, nohow. But I got even with him: I pisoned HIS dog." His clumsy utterance, his rude embarrassed manner, set a fresh value on the stupidity of his remarks. I do not think I ever appreciated the meaning of two words until I knew Irvine--the verb, loaf, and the noun, oaf; between them, they complete his portrait. He could lounge, and wriggle, and rub himself against the wall, and grin, and be more in everybody's way than any other two people that I ever set my eyes on. Nothing that he did became him; and yet you were conscious that he was one of your own race, that his mind was cumbrously at work, revolving the problem of existence like a quid of gum, and in his own cloudy manner enjoying life, and passing judgment on his fellows. Above all things, he was delighted with himself. You would not have thought it, from his uneasy manners and troubled, struggling utterance; but he loved himself to the marrow, and was happy and proud like a peacock on a rail.

His self-esteem was, indeed, the one joint in his harness. He could be got to work, and even kept at work, by flattery. As long as my wife stood over him, crying out how strong he was, so long exactly he would stick to the matter in hand; and the moment she turned her back, or ceased to praise him, he would stop. His physical strength was wonderful; and to have a woman stand by and admire his achievements, warmed his heart like sunshine. Yet he was as cowardly as he was powerful, and felt no shame in owning to the weakness. Something was once wanted from the crazy platform over the shaft, and he at once refused to venture there--"did not like," as he said, "foolen' round them kind o' places," and let my wife go instead of him, looking on with a grin. Vanity, where it rules, is usually more heroic: but Irvine steadily approved himself, and expected others to approve him; rather looked down upon my wife, and decidedly expected her to look up to him, on the strength of his superior prudence.

Yet the strangest part of the whole matter was perhaps this, that Irvine was as beautiful as a statue. His features were, in themselves, perfect; it was only his cloudy, uncouth, and coarse expression that disfigured them. So much strength residing in so spare a frame was proof sufficient of the accuracy of his shape. He must have been built somewhat after the pattern of Jack Sheppard; but the famous housebreaker, we may be certain, was no lout. It was by the extraordinary powers of his mind no less than by the vigour of his body, that he broke his strong prison with such imperfect implements, turning the very obstacles to service. Irvine, in the same case, would have sat down and spat, and grumbled curses. He had the soul of a fat sheep, but, regarded as an artist's model, the exterior of a Greek God. It was a cruel thought to persons less favoured in their birth, that this creature, endowed--to use the language of theatres--with extraordinary "means," should so manage to misemploy them that he looked ugly and almost deformed. It was only by an effort of abstraction, and after many days, that you discovered what he was.

By playing on the oaf's conceit, and standing closely over him, we got a path made round the corner of the dump to our door, so that we could come and go with decent ease; and he even enjoyed the work, for in that there were boulders to be plucked up bodily, bushes to be uprooted, and other occasions for athletic display: but cutting wood was a different matter. Anybody could cut wood; and, besides, my wife was tired of supervising him, and had other things to attend to. And, in short, days went by, and Irvine came daily, and talked and lounged and spat; but the firewood remained intact as sleepers on the platform or growing trees upon the mountainside. Irvine, as a woodcutter, we could tolerate; but Irvine as a friend of the family, at so much a day, was too bald an imposition, and at length, on the afternoon of the fourth or fifth day of our connection, I explained to him, as clearly as I could, the light in which I had grown to regard his presence. I pointed out to him that I could not continue to give him a salary for spitting on the floor; and this expression, which came after a good many others, at last penetrated his obdurate wits. He rose at once, and said if that was the way he was going to be spoke to, he reckoned he would quit. And, no one interposing, he departed.

So far, so good. But we had no firewood. The next afternoon, I strolled down to Rufe's and consulted him on the subject. It was a very droll interview, in the large, bare north room of the Silverado Hotel, Mrs. Hanson's patchwork on a frame, and Rufe, and his wife, and I, and the oaf himself, all more or less embarrassed. Rufe announced there was nobody in the neighbourhood but Irvine who could do a day's work for anybody. Irvine, thereupon, refused to have any more to do with my service; he "wouldn't work no more for a man as had spoke to him's I had done." I found myself on the point of the last humiliation--driven to beseech the creature whom I had just dismissed with insult: but I took the high hand in despair, said there must be no talk of Irvine coming back unless matters were to be differently managed; that I would rather chop firewood for myself than be fooled; and, in short, the Hansons being eager for the lad's hire, I so imposed upon them with merely affected resolution, that they ended by begging me to re-employ him again, on a solemn promise that he should be more industrious. The promise, I am bound to say, was kept. We soon had a fine pile of firewood at our door; and if Caliban gave me the cold shoulder and spared me his conversation, I thought none the worse of him for that, nor did I find my days much longer for the deprivation.

The leading spirit of the family was, I am inclined to fancy, Mrs. Hanson. Her social brilliancy somewhat dazzled the others, and she had more of the small change of sense. It was she who faced Kelmar, for instance; and perhaps, if she had been alone, Kelmar would have had no rule within her doors. Rufe, to be sure, had a fine, sober, open-air attitude of mind, seeing the world without exaggeration--perhaps, we may even say, without enough; for he lacked, along with the others, that commercial idealism which puts so high a value on time and money. Sanity itself is a kind of convention. Perhaps Rufe was wrong; but, looking on life plainly, he was unable to perceive that croquet or poker were in any way less important than, for instance, mending his waggon. Even his own profession, hunting, was dear to him mainly as a sort of play; even that he would have neglected, had it not appealed to his imagination. His hunting-suit, for instance, had cost I should be afraid to say how many bucks--the currency in which he paid his way: it was all befringed, after the Indian fashion, and it was dear to his heart. The pictorial side of his daily business was never forgotten. He was even anxious to stand for his picture in those buckskin hunting clothes; and I remember how he once warmed almost into enthusiasm, his dark blue eyes growing perceptibly larger, as he planned the composition in which he should appear, "with the horns of some real big bucks, and dogs, and a camp on a crick" (creek, stream).

There was no trace in Irvine of this woodland poetry. He did not care for hunting, nor yet for buckskin suits. He had never observed scenery. The world, as it appeared to him, was almost obliterated by his own great grinning figure in the foreground: Caliban Malvolio. And it seems to me as if, in the persons of these brothers-in-law, we had the two sides of rusticity fairly well represented: the hunter living really in nature; the clodhopper living merely out of society: the one bent up in every corporal agent to capacity in one pursuit, doing at least one thing keenly and thoughtfully, and thoroughly alive to all that touches it; the other in the inert and bestial state, walking in a faint dream, and taking so dim an impression of the myriad sides of life that he is truly conscious of nothing but himself. It is only in the fastnesses of nature, forests, mountains, and the back of man's beyond, that a creature endowed with five senses can grow up into the perfection of this crass and earthy vanity. In towns or the busier country sides, he is roughly reminded of other men's existence; and if he learns no more, he learns at least to fear contempt. But Irvine had come scatheless through life, conscious only of himself, of his great strength and intelligence; and in the silence of the universe, to which he did not listen, dwelling with delight on the sound of his own thoughts.

THE SEA FOGS

A change in the colour of the light usually called me in the morning. By a certain hour, the long, vertical chinks in our western gable, where the boards had shrunk and separated, flashed suddenly into my eyes as stripes of dazzling blue, at once so dark and splendid that I used to marvel how the qualities could be combined. At an earlier hour, the heavens in that quarter were still quietly coloured, but the shoulder of the mountain which shuts in the canyon already glowed with sunlight in a wonderful compound of gold and rose and green; and this too would kindle, although more mildly and with rainbow tints, the fissures of our crazy gable. If I were sleeping heavily, it was the bold blue that struck me awake; if more lightly, then I would come to myself in that earlier and fairier fight.

One Sunday morning, about five, the first brightness called me. I rose and turned to the east, not for my devotions, but for air. The night had been very still. The little private gale that blew every evening in our canyon, for ten minutes or perhaps a quarter of an hour, had swiftly blown itself out; in the hours that followed not a sigh of wind had shaken the treetops; and our barrack, for all its breaches, was less fresh that morning than of wont. But I had no sooner reached the window than I forgot all else in the sight that met my eyes, and I made but two bounds into my clothes, and down the crazy plank to the platform.

The sun was still concealed below the opposite hilltops, though it was shining already, not twenty feet above my head, on our own mountain slope. But the scene, beyond a few near features, was entirely changed. Napa valley was gone; gone were all the lower slopes and woody foothills of the range; and in their place, not a thousand feet below me, rolled a great level ocean. It was as though I had gone to bed the night before, safe in a nook of inland mountains, and had awakened in a bay upon the coast. I had seen these inundations from below; at Calistoga I had risen and gone abroad in the early morning, coughing and sneezing, under fathoms on fathoms of gray sea vapour, like a cloudy sky--a dull sight for the artist, and a painful experience for the invalid. But to sit aloft one's self in the pure air and under the unclouded dome of heaven, and thus look down on the submergence of the valley, was strangely different and even delightful to the eyes. Far away were hilltops like little islands. Nearer, a smoky surf beat about the foot of precipices and poured into all the coves of these rough mountains. The colour of that fog ocean was a thing never to be forgotten. For an instant, among the Hebrides and just about sundown, I have seen something like it on the sea itself. But the white was not so opaline; nor was there, what surprisingly increased the effect, that breathless, crystal stillness over all. Even in its gentlest moods the salt sea travails, moaning among the weeds or lisping on the sand; but that vast fog ocean lay in a trance of silence, nor did the sweet air of the morning tremble with a sound.

As I continued to sit upon the dump, I began to observe that this sea was not so level as at first sight it appeared to be. Away in the extreme south, a little hill of fog arose against the sky above the general surface, and as it had already caught the sun, it shone on the horizon like the topsails of some giant ship. There were huge waves, stationary, as it seemed, like waves in a frozen sea; and yet, as I looked again, I was not sure but they were moving after all, with a slow and august advance. And while I was yet doubting, a promontory of the some four or five miles away, conspicuous by a bouquet of tall pines, was in a single instant overtaken and swallowed up. It re-appeared in a little, with its pines, but this time as an islet, and only to be swallowed up once more and then for good. This set me looking nearer, and I saw that in every cove along the line of mountains the fog was being piled in higher and higher, as though by some wind that was inaudible to me. I could trace its progress, one pine tree first growing hazy and then disappearing after another; although sometimes there was none of this fore-running haze, but the whole opaque white ocean gave a start and swallowed a piece of mountain at a gulp. It was to flee these poisonous fogs that I had left the seaboard, and climbed so high among the mountains. And now, behold, here came the fog to besiege me in my chosen altitudes, and yet came so beautifully that my first thought was of welcome.

The sun had now gotten much higher, and through all the gaps of the hills it cast long bars of gold across that white ocean. An eagle, or some other very great bird of the mountain, came wheeling over the nearer pine-tops, and hung, poised and something sideways, as if to look abroad on that unwonted desolation, spying, perhaps with terror, for the eyries of her comrades. Then, with a long cry, she dis-appeared again towards Lake County and the clearer air. At length it seemed to me as if the flood were beginning to subside. The old landmarks, by whose disappear-ance I had measured its advance, here a crag, there a brave pine tree, now began, in the inverse order, to make their reappearance into daylight. I judged all danger of the fog was over. This was not Noah's flood; it was but a morning spring, and would now drift out seaward whence it came. So, mightily relieved, and a good deal ex-hilarated by the sight, I went into the house to light the fire.

I suppose it was nearly seven when I once more mounted the platform to look abroad. The fog ocean had swelled up enormously since last I saw it; and a few hundred feet below me, in the deep gap where the Toll House stands and the road runs through into Lake County, it had already topped the slope, and was pouring over and down the other side like driving smoke. The wind had climbed along with it; and though I was still in calm air, I could see the trees tossing below me, and their long, strident sighing mounted to me where I stood.

Half an hour later, the fog had surmounted all the ridge on the opposite side of the gap, though a shoulder of the mountain still warded it out of our canyon. Napa valley and its bounding hills were now utterly blotted out. The fog, sunny white in the sunshine, was pouring over into Lake County in a huge, ragged cataract, tossing treetops appearing and disappearing in the spray. The air struck with a little chill, and set me coughing. It smelt strong of the fog, like the smell of a washing-house, but with a shrewd tang of the sea salt.

Had it not been for two things--the sheltering spur which answered as a dyke, and the great valley on the other side which rapidly engulfed whatever mounted-- our own little platform in the canyon must have been already buried a hundred feet in salt and poisonous air. As it was, the interest of the scene entirely occupied our minds. We were set just out of the wind, and but just above the fog; we could listen to the voice of the one as to music on the stage; we could plunge our eyes down into the other, as into some flowing stream from over the parapet of a bridge; thus we looked on upon a strange, impetuous, silent, shifting exhibition of the powers of nature, and saw the familiar landscape changing from moment to moment like figures in a dream.

The imagination loves to trifle with what is not. Had this been indeed the deluge, I should have felt more strongly, but the emotion would have been similar in kind. I played with the idea, as the child flees in delighted terror from the creations of his fancy. The look of the thing helped me. And when at last I began to flee up the mountain, it was indeed partly to escape from the raw air that kept me coughing, but it was also part in play.

As I ascended the mountain-side, I came once more to overlook the upper surface of the fog; but it wore a different appearance from what I had beheld at daybreak. For, first, the sun now fell on it from high overhead, and its surface shone and undulated like a great nor'land moor country, sheeted with untrodden morning snow. And next the new level must have been a thousand or fifteen hundred feet higher than the old, so that only five or six points of all the broken country below me, still stood out. Napa valley was now one with Sonoma on the west. On the hither side, only a thin scattered fringe of bluffs was unsubmerged; and through all the gaps the fog was pouring over, like an ocean, into the blue clear sunny country on the east. There it was soon lost; for it fell instantly into the bottom of the valleys, following the water-shed; and the hilltops in that quarter were still clear cut upon the eastern sky.

Through the Toll House gap and over the near ridges on the other side, the deluge was immense. A spray of thin vapour was thrown high above it, rising and falling, and blown into fantastic shapes. The speed of its course was like a mountain torrent. Here and there a few treetops were discovered and then whelmed again; and for one second, the bough of a dead pine beckoned out of the spray like the arm of a drowning man. But still the imagination was dissatisfied, still the ear waited for something more. Had this indeed been water (as it seemed so, to the eye), with what a plunge of reverberating thunder would it have rolled upon its course, disembowelling mountains and deracinating pines! And yet water it was, and sea-water at that--true Pacific billows, only somewhat rarefied, rolling in mid air among the hilltops.

I climbed still higher, among the red rattling gravel and dwarf underwood of Mount Saint Helena, until I could look right down upon Silverado, and admire the favoured nook in which it lay. The sunny plain of fog was several hundred feet higher; behind the protecting spur a gigantic accumulation of cottony vapour threatened, with every second, to blow over and submerge our homestead; but the vortex setting past the Toll House was too strong; and there lay our little platform, in the arms of the deluge, but still enjoying its unbroken sunshine. About eleven, however, thin spray came flying over the friendly buttress, and I began to think the fog had hunted out its Jonah after all. But it was the last effort. The wind veered while we were at dinner, and began to blow squally from the mountain summit; and by half-past one, all that world of sea- fogs was utterly routed and flying here and there into the south in little rags of cloud. And instead of a lone sea-beach, we found ourselves once more inhabiting a high mountainside, with the clear green country far below us, and the light smoke of Calistoga blowing in the air.

This was the great Russian campaign for that season. Now and then, in the early morning, a little white lakelet of fog would be seen far down in Napa Valley; but the heights were not again assailed, nor was the surrounding world again shut off from Silverado.

THE TOLL HOUSE

The Toll House, standing alone by the wayside under nodding pines, with its streamlet and water-tank; its backwoods, toll-bar, and well trodden croquet ground; the ostler standing by the stable door, chewing a straw; a glimpse of the Chinese cook in the back parts; and Mr. Hoddy in the bar, gravely alert and serviceable, and equally anxious to lend or borrow books;--dozed all day in the dusty sunshine, more than half asleep. There were no neighbours, except the Hansons up the hill. The traffic on the road was infinitesimal; only, at rare intervals, a couple in a wag-gon, or a dusty farmer on a springboard, toiling over "the grade" to that metropoli-tan hamlet, Calistoga; and, at the fixed hours, the passage of the stages.

The nearest building was the school-house, down the road; and the school-ma'am boarded at the Toll House, walking thence in the morning to the little brown shanty, where she taught the young ones of the district, and returning thither pret-ty weary in the afternoon. She had chosen this outlying situation, I understood, for her health. Mr. Corwin was consumptive; so was Rufe; so was Mr. Jennings, the engineer. In short, the place was a kind of small Davos: consumptive folk consort-ing on a hilltop in the most unbroken idleness. Jennings never did anything that I could see, except now and then to fish, and generally to sit about in the bar and the verandah, waiting for something to happen. Corwin and Rufe did as little as pos-sible; and if the school-ma'am, poor lady, had to work pretty hard all morning, she subsided when it was over into much the same dazed beatitude as all the rest.

Her special corner was the parlour--a very genteel room, with Bible prints, a crayon portrait of Mrs. Corwin in the height of fashion, a few years ago, another of her son (Mr. Corwin was not represented), a mirror, and a selection of dried grasses. A large book was laid religiously on the table--"From Palace to Hovel," I believe, its name--full of the raciest experiences in England. The author had mingled freely with all classes, the nobility particularly meeting him with open arms; and I must say that traveller had ill requited his reception. His book, in short, was a capital instance of the Penny Messalina school of literature; and there arose from it, in that cool parlour, in that silent, wayside, mountain inn, a rank atmosphere of gold and blood and "Jenkins," and the "Mysteries of London," and sickening, inverted snobbery, fit to knock you down. The mention of this book reminds me of another and far racier picture of our island life. The latter parts of Rocambole are surely too sparingly consulted in the country which they celebrate. No man's education can be said to be complete, nor can he pronounce the world yet emptied of enjoyment, till he has made the acquaintance of "the Reverend Patterson, director of the Evangelical Society." To follow the evolutions of that reverend gentleman, who goes through scenes in which even Mr. Duffield would hesitate to place a bishop, is to rise to new ideas. But, alas! there was no Patterson about the Toll House. Only, alongside of "From Palace to Hovel," a sixpenny "Ouida" figured. So literature, you see, was not unrepresented.

The school-ma'am had friends to stay with her, other school-ma'ams enjoying their holidays, quite a bevy of damsels. They seemed never to go out, or not beyond the verandah, but sat close in the little parlour, quietly talking or listening to the wind among the trees. Sleep dwelt in the Toll House, like a fixture: summer sleep, shallow, soft, and dreamless. A cuckoo-clock, a great rarity in such a place, hooted at intervals about the echoing house; and Mr. Jenning would open his eyes for a moment in the bar, and turn the leaf of a newspaper, and the resting school-ma'ams in the parlour would be recalled to the consciousness of their inaction. Busy Mrs. Corwin and her busy Chinaman might be heard indeed, in the penetralia, pounding dough or rattling dishes; or perhaps Rufe had called up some of the sleepers for a game of croquet, and the hollow strokes of the mallet sounded far away among the woods: but with these exceptions, it was sleep and sunshine and dust, and the wind in the pine trees, all day long.

A little before stage time, that castle of indolence awoke. The ostler threw his straw away and set to his preparations. Mr. Jennings rubbed his eyes; happy Mr. Jennings, the something he had been waiting for all day about to happen at last! The boarders gathered in the verandah, silently giving ear, and gazing down the road with shaded eyes. And as yet there was no sign for the senses, not a sound, not a tremor of the mountain road. The birds, to whom the secret of the hooting cuckoo is unknown, must have set down to instinct this premonitory bustle.

And then the first of the two stages swooped upon the Toll House with a roar and in a cloud of dust; and the shock had not yet time to subside, before the second was abreast of it. Huge concerns they were, well-horsed and loaded, the men in their shirt-sleeves, the women swathed in veils, the long whip cracking like a pistol; and as they charged upon that slumbering hostelry, each shepherding a dust storm, the dead place blossomed into life and talk and clatter. This the Toll House?--with its city throng, its jostling shoulders, its infinity of instant business in the bar? The mind would not receive it! The heartfelt bustle of that hour is hardly credible; the thrill of the great shower of letters from the post- bag, the childish hope and inter-est with which one gazed in all these strangers' eyes. They paused there but to pass: the blue- clad China-boy, the San Francisco magnate, the mystery in the dust coat, the secret memoirs in tweed, the ogling, well-shod lady with her troop of girls; they did but flash and go; they were hull-down for us behind life's ocean, and we but hailed their topsails on the line. Yet, out of our great solitude of four and twen-ty mountain hours, we thrilled to their momentary presence gauged and divined them, loved and hated; and stood light-headed in that storm of human electricity. Yes, like Piccadilly circus, this is also one of life's crossing-places. Here I beheld one man, already famous or infamous, a centre of pistol-shots: and another who, if not yet known to rumour, will fill a column of the Sunday paper when he comes to hang--a burly, thick-set, powerful Chinese desperado, six long bristles upon either lip; redolent of whiskey, playing cards, and pistols; swaggering in the bar with the lowest assumption of the lowest European manners; rapping out blackguard English oaths in his canorous oriental voice; and combining in one person the depravities of two races and two civilizations. For all his lust and vigour, he seemed to look cold upon me from the valley of the shadow of the gallows. He imagined a vain thing; and while he drained his cock-tail, Holbein's death was at his elbow. Once, too, I fell in talk with another of these flitting strangers--like the rest, in his shirt-sleeves and all begrimed with dust--and the next minute we were discussing Paris and Lon-don, theatres and wines. To him, journeying from one human place to another, this was a trifle; but to me! No, Mr. Lillie, I have not forgotten it.

And presently the city-tide was at its flood and began to ebb. Life runs in Picca-dilly Circus, say, from nine to one, and then, there also, ebbs into the small hours of the echoing policeman and the lamps and stars. But the Toll House is far up stream, and near its rural springs; the bubble of the tide but touches it. Before you had yet grasped your pleasure, the horses were put to, the loud whips volleyed, and the tide was gone. North and south had the two stages vanished, the towering dust subsided in the woods; but there was still an interval before the flush had fallen on your cheeks, before the ear became once more contented with the silence, or the seven sleepers of the Toll House dozed back to their accustomed corners. Yet a little, and the ostler would swing round the great barrier across the road; and in the golden evening, that dreamy inn begin to trim its lamps and spread the board for supper.

As I recall the place--the green dell below; the spires of pine; the sun-warm, scented air; that gray, gabled inn, with its faint stirrings of life amid the slumber of the mountains--I slowly awake to a sense of admiration, gratitude, and almost love. A fine place, after all, for a wasted life to doze away in--the cuckoo clock hooting of its far home country; the croquet mallets, eloquent of English lawns; the stages daily bringing news of--the turbulent world away below there; and perhaps once in the summer, a salt fog pouring overhead with its tale of the Pacific.

A STARRY DRIVE

In our rule at Silverado, there was a melancholy interregnum. The queen and the crown prince with one accord fell sick; and, as I was sick to begin with, our lone position on Mount Saint Helena was no longer tenable, and we had to hurry back to Calistoga and a cottage on the green. By that time we had begun to realize the difficulties of our position. We had found what an amount of labour it cost to support life in our red canyon; and it was the dearest desire of our hearts to get a China-boy to go along with us when we returned. We could have given him a whole house to himself, self-contained, as they say in the advertisements; and on the money question we were prepared to go far. Kong Sam Kee, the Calistoga washerman, was entrusted with the affair; and from day to day it languished on, with protestations on our part and mellifluous excuses on the part of Kong Sam Kee.

At length, about half-past eight of our last evening, with the waggon ready harnessed to convey us up the grade, the washerman, with a somewhat sneering air, produced the boy. He was a handsome, gentlemanly lad, attired in rich dark blue, and shod with snowy white; but, alas! he had heard rumours of Silverado. He know it for a lone place on the mountain-side, with no friendly wash-house near by, where he might smoke a pipe of opium o' nights with other China-boys, and lose his little earnings at the game of tan; and he first backed out for more money; and then, when that demand was satisfied, refused to come point-blank. He was wedded to his wash- houses; he had no taste for the rural life; and we must go to our mountain servantless. It must have been near half an hour before we reached that conclusion, standing in the midst of Calistoga high street under the stars, and the China-boy and Kong Sam Kee singing their pigeon English in the sweetest voices and with the most musical inflections.

We were not, however, to return alone; for we brought with us Joe Strong, the painter, a most good-natured comrade and a capital hand at an omelette. I do not know in which capacity he was most valued--as a cook or a companion; and he did excellently well in both.

The Kong Sam Kee negotiation had delayed us unduly; it must have been half-past nine before we left Calistoga, and night came fully ere we struck the bottom of the grade. I have never seen such a night. It seemed to throw calumny in the teeth of all the painters that ever dabbled in starlight. The sky itself was of a ruddy, powerful, nameless, changing colour, dark and glossy like a serpent's back. The stars, by innumerable millions, stuck boldly forth like lamps. The milky way was bright, like a moonlit cloud; half heaven seemed milky way. The greater luminaries shone each more clearly than a winter's moon. Their light was dyed in every sort of colour--red, like fire; blue, like steel; green, like the tracks of sunset; and so sharply did each stand forth in its own lustre that there was no appearance of that flat, star-spangled arch we know so well in pictures, but all the hollow of heaven was one chaos of contesting luminaries--a hurry-burly of stars. Against this the hills and rugged treetops stood out redly dark.

As we continued to advance, the lesser lights and milky ways first grew pale, and then vanished; the countless hosts of heaven dwindled in number by successive millions; those that still shone had tempered their exceeding brightness and fallen back into their customary wistful distance; and the sky declined from its first bewildering splendour into the appearance of a common night. Slowly this change proceeded, and still there was no sign of any cause. Then a whiteness like mist was thrown over the spurs of the mountain. Yet a while, and, as we turned a corner, a great leap of silver light and net of forest shadows fell across the road and upon our wondering waggonful; and, swimming low among the trees, we beheld a strange, misshapen, waning moon, half-tilted on her back.

"Where are ye when the moon appears?" so the old poet sang, half- taunting, to the stars, bent upon a courtly purpose.

"As the sunlight round the dim earth's midnight tower of shadow pours, Streaming past the dim, wide portals, Viewless to the eyes of mortals, Till it floods the moon's pale islet or the morning's golden shores."

So sings Mr. Trowbridge, with a noble inspiration. And so had the sunlight flooded that pale islet of the moon, and her lit face put out, one after another, that galaxy of stars. The wonder of the drive was over; but, by some nice conjunction of clearness in the air and fit shadow in the valley where we travelled, we had seen for a little while that brave display of the midnight heavens. It was gone, but it had been; nor shall I ever again behold the stars with the same mind. He who has seen the sea commoved with a great hurricane, thinks of it very differently from him who has seen it only in a calm. And the difference between a calm and a hurricane is not greatly more striking than that between the ordinary face of night and the splendour that shone upon us in that drive. Two in our waggon knew night as she shines upon the tropics, but even that bore no comparison. The nameless colour of the sky, the hues of the star-fire, and the incredible projection of the stars themselves, starting from their orbits, so that the eye seemed to distinguish their positions in the hollow of space--these were things that we had never seen before and shall never see again.

Meanwhile, in this altered night, we proceeded on our way among the scents and silence of the forest, reached the top of the grade, wound up by Hanson's, and came at last to a stand under the flying gargoyle of the chute. Sam, who had been lying back, fast asleep, with the moon on his face, got down, with the remark that it was pleasant "to be home." The waggon turned and drove away, the noise gently dying in the woods, and we clambered up the rough path, Caliban's great feat of engineering, and came home to Silverado.

The moon shone in at the eastern doors and windows, and over the lumber on the platform. The one tall pine beside. the ledge was steeped in silver. Away up the canyon, a wild cat welcomed us with three discordant squalls. But once we had lit a candle, and began to review our improvements, homely in either sense, and count our stores, it was wonderful what a feeling of possession and permanence grow up in the hearts of the lords of Silverado. A bed had still to be made up for Strong, and the morning's water to be fetched, with clinking pail; and as we set about these household duties, and showed off our wealth and conveniences before the stranger, and had a glass of wine, I think, in honour of our return, and trooped at length one after another up the flying bridge of plank, and lay down to sleep in our shattered, moon- pierced barrack, we were among the happiest sovereigns in the world, and certainly ruled over the most contented people. Yet, in our absence, the palace had been sacked. Wild cats, so the Hansons said, had broken in and carried off a side of bacon, a hatchet, and two knives.

EPISODES IN THE STORY OF A MINE

No one could live at Silverado and not be curious about the story of the mine. We were surrounded by so many evidences of expense and toil, we lived so entirely in the wreck of that great enterprise, like mites in the ruins of a cheese, that the idea of the old din and bustle haunted our repose. Our own house, the forge, the dump, the chutes, the rails, the windlass, the mass of broken plant; the two tunnels, one far below in the green dell, the other on the platform where we kept our wine; the deep shaft, with the sun-glints and the water-drops; above all, the ledge, that great gaping slice out of the mountain shoulder, propped apart by wooden wedges, on whose immediate margin, high above our heads, the one tall pine precariously nodded--these stood for its greatness; while, the dog-hutch, boot-jacks, old boots, old tavern bills, and the very beds that we inherited from bygone miners, put in human touches and realized for us the story of the past.

I have sat on an old sleeper, under the thick madronas near the forge, with just a look over the dump on the green world below, and seen the sun lying broad among the wreck, and heard the silence broken only by the tinkling water in the shaft, or a stir of the royal family about the battered palace, and my mind has gone back to the epoch of the Stanleys and the Chapmans, with a grand tutti of pick and drill, hammer and anvil, echoing about the canyon; the assayer hard at it in our dining-room; the carts below on the road, and their cargo of red mineral bounding and thundering down the iron chute. And now all gone--all fallen away into this sunny silence and desertion: a family of squatters dining in the assayer's office, making their beds in the big sleeping room erstwhile so crowded, keeping their wine in the tunnel that once rang with picks.

But Silverado itself, although now fallen in its turn into decay, was once but a mushroom, and had succeeded to other mines and other flitting cities. Twenty years ago, away down the glen on the Lake County side there was a place, Jonestown by name, with two thousand inhabitants dwelling under canvas, and one roofed house for the sale of whiskey. Round on the western side of Mount Saint Helena, there was at the same date, a second large encampment, its name, if it ever had one, lost for me. Both of these have perished, leaving not a stick and scarce a memory behind them. Tide after tide of hopeful miners have thus flowed and ebbed about the mountain, coming and going, now by lone prospectors, now with a rush. Last, in order of time came Silverado, reared the big mill, in the valley, founded the town which is now represented, monumentally, by Hanson's, pierced all these slaps and shafts and tunnels, and in turn declined and died away.

"Our noisy years seem moments in the wake Of the eternal silence."

As to the success of Silverado in its time of being, two reports were current. According to the first, six hundred thousand dollars were taken out of that great upright seam, that still hung open above us on crazy wedges. Then the ledge pinched out, and there followed, in quest of the remainder, a great drifting and tunnelling in all directions, and a great consequent effusion of dollars, until, all parties being sick of the expense, the mine was deserted, and the town decamped. According to the second version, told me with much secrecy of manner, the whole affair, mine, mill, and town, were parts of one majestic swindle. There had never come any silver out of any portion of the mine; there was no silver to come. At midnight trains of packhorses might have been observed winding by devious tracks about the shoulder of the mountain. They came from far away, from Amador or Placer, laden with silver in "old cigar boxes." They discharged their load at Silverado, in the hour of sleep; and before the morning they were gone again with their mysterious drivers to their unknown source. In this way, twenty thousand pounds' worth of silver was smuggled in under cover of night, in these old cigar boxes; mixed with Silverado mineral; carted down to the mill; crushed, amalgated, and refined, and despatched to the city as the proper product of the mine. Stock- jobbing, if it can cover such expenses, must be a profitable business in San Francisco.

I give these two versions as I got them. But I place little reliance on either, my belief in history having been greatly shaken. For it chanced that I had come to dwell in Silverado at a critical hour; great events in its history were about to happen-- did happen, as I am led to believe; nay, and it will be seen that I played a part in that revolution myself. And yet from first to last I never had a glimmer of an idea what was going on; and even now, after full reflection, profess myself at sea. That there was some obscure intrigue of the cigar-box order, and that I, in the character of a wooden puppet, set pen to paper in the interest of somebody, so much, and no more, is certain.

Silverado, then under my immediate sway, belonged to one whom I will call a Mr. Ronalds. I only knew him through the extraordinarily distorting medium of local gossip, now as a momentous jobber; now as a dupe to point an adage; and again, and much more probably, as an ordinary Christian gentleman like you or me, who had opened a mine and worked it for a while with better and worse fortune. So, through a defective window-pane, you may see the passer-by shoot up into a hunchbacked giant or dwindle into a potbellied dwarf.

To Ronalds, at least, the mine belonged; but the notice by which he held it would ran out upon the 30th of June--or rather, as I suppose, it had run out already, and the month of grace would expire upon that day, after which any American citizen might post a notice of his own, and make Silverado his. This, with a sort of quiet slyness, Rufe told me at an early period of our acquaintance. There was no silver, of course; the mine "wasn't worth nothing, Mr. Stevens," but there was a deal of old iron and wood around, and to gain possession of this old wood and iron, and get a right to the water, Rufe proposed, if I had no objections, to "jump the claim."

Of course, I had no objection. But I was filled with wonder. If all he wanted was the wood and iron, what, in the name of fortune, was to prevent him taking them? "His right there was none to dispute." He might lay hands on all to-morrow, as the wild cats had laid hands upon our knives and hatchet. Besides, was this mass of heavy mining plant worth transportation? If it was, why had not the rightful owners carted it away? If it was, would they not preserve their title to these movables, even after they had lost their title to the mine? And if it were not, what the better was Rufe? Nothing would grow at Silverado; there was even no wood to cut; beyond a sense of property, there was nothing to be gained. Lastly, was it at all credible that Ronalds would forget what Rufe remembered? The days of grace were not yet over: any fine morning he might appear, paper in hand, and enter for another year on his inheritance. However, it was none of my business; all seemed legal; Rufe or Ronalds, all was one to me.

On the morning of the 27th, Mrs. Hanson appeared with the milk as usual, in her sun-bonnet. The time would be out on Tuesday, she reminded us, and bade me be in readiness to play my part, though I had no idea what it was to be. And suppose Ronalds came? we asked. She received the idea with derision, laughing aloud with all her fine teeth. He could not find the mine to save his life, it appeared, without Rufe to guide him. Last year, when he came, they heard him "up and down the road a hollerin' and a raisin' Cain." And at last he had to come to the Hansons in despair, and bid Rufe, "Jump into your pants and shoes, and show me where this old mine is, anyway!" Seeing that Ronalds had laid out so much money in the spot, and that a beaten road led right up to the bottom of the clump, I thought this a remarkable example. The sense of locality must be singularly in abeyance in the case of Ronalds.

That same evening, supper comfortably over, Joe Strong busy at work on a drawing of the dump and the opposite hills, we were all out on the platform together, sitting there, under the tented heavens, with the same sense of privacy as if we had been cabined in a parlour, when the sound of brisk footsteps came mounting up the path. We pricked our ears at this, for the tread seemed lighter and firmer than was usual with our country neighbours. And presently, sure enough, two town gentlemen, with cigars and kid gloves, came debauching past the house. They looked in that place like a blasphemy.

"Good evening," they said. For none of us had stirred; we all sat stiff with wonder.

"Good evening," I returned; and then, to put them at their ease, "A stiff climb," I added.

"Yes," replied the leader; "but we have to thank you for this path."

I did not like the man's tone. None of us liked it. He did not seem embarrassed by the meeting, but threw us his remarks like favours, and strode magisterially by us towards the shaft and tunnel.

Presently we heard his voice raised to his companion. "We drifted every sort of way, but couldn't strike the ledge." Then again: "It pinched out here." And once more: "Every minor that ever worked upon it says there's bound to be a ledge somewhere."

These were the snatches of his talk that reached us, and they had a damning significance. We, the lords of Silverado, had come face to face with our superior. It is the worst of all quaint and of all cheap ways of life that they bring us at last to the pinch of some humiliation. I liked well enough to be a squatter when there was none but Hanson by; before Ronalds, I will own, I somewhat quailed. I hastened to do him fealty, said I gathered he was the Squattee, and apologized. He threatened me with ejection, in a manner grimly pleasant--more pleasant to him, I fancy, than to me; and then he passed off into praises of the former state of Silverado. "It was the busiest little mining town you ever saw:" a population of between a thousand and fifteen hundred souls, the engine in full blast, the mill newly erected; nothing going but champagne, and hope the order of the day. Ninety thousand dollars came out; a hundred and forty thousand were put in, making a net loss of fifty thousand. The last days, I gathered, the days of John Stanley, were not so bright; the champagne had ceased to flow, the population was already moving elsewhere, and Silverado had begun to wither in the branch before it was cut at the root. The last shot that was fired knocked over the stove chimney, and made that hole in the roof of our barrack, through which the sun was wont to visit slug-a-beds towards afternoon. A noisy, last shot, to inaugurate the days of silence.

Throughout this interview, my conscience was a good deal exercised; and I was moved to throw myself on my knees and own the intended treachery. But then I had Hanson to consider. I was in much the same position as Old Rowley, that royal humourist, whom "the rogue had taken into his confidence." And again, here was Ronalds on the spot. He must know the day of the month as well as Hanson and I. If a broad hint were necessary, he had the broadest in the world. For a large board had been nailed by the crown prince on the very front of our house, between the door and window, painted in cinnabar--the pigment of the country--with doggrel rhymes and contumelious pictures, and announcing, in terms unnecessarily figurative, that the trick was already played, the claim already jumped, and Master Sam the legitimate successor of Mr. Ronalds. But no, nothing could save that man; quem deus vult perdere, prius dementat. As he came so he went, and left his rights depending.

Late at night, by Silverado reckoning, and after we were all abed, Mrs. Hanson returned to give us the newest of her news. It was like a scene in a ship's steerage: all of us abed in our different tiers, the single candle struggling with the darkness, and this plump, handsome woman, seated on an upturned valise beside the bunks, talking and showing her fine teeth, and laughing till the rafters rang. Any ship, to be sure, with a hundredth part as many holes in it as our barrack, must long ago have gone to her last port. Up to that time I had always imagined Mrs. Hanson's loquacity to be mere incontinence, that she said what was uppermost for the pleasure of speaking, and laughed and laughed again as a kind of musical accompaniment. But I now found there was an art in it, I found it less communicative than silence itself. I wished to know why Ronalds had come; how he had found his way without Rufe; and why, being on the spot, he had not refreshed his title. She talked interminably on, but her replies were never answers. She fled under a cloud of words; and when I had made sure that she was purposely eluding me, I dropped the subject in my turn, and let her rattle where she would.

She had come to tell us that, instead of waiting for Tuesday, the claim was to be jumped on the morrow. How? If the time were not out, it was impossible. Why? If Ronalds had come and gone, and done nothing, there was the less cause for hurry. But again I could reach no satisfaction. The claim was to be jumped next morning, that was all that she would condescend upon.

And yet it was not jumped the next morning, nor yet the next, and a whole week had come and gone before we heard more of this exploit. That day week, however, a day of great heat, Hanson, with a little roll of paper in his hand, and the eternal pipe alight; Breedlove, his large, dull friend, to act, I suppose, as witness; Mrs. Hanson, in her Sunday best; and all the children, from the oldest to the youngest;--arrived in a procession, tailing one behind another up the path. Caliban was absent, but he had been chary of his friendly visits since the row; and with that exception, the whole family was gathered together as for a marriage or a christening. Strong was sitting at work, in the shade of the dwarf madronas near the forge; and they planted themselves about him in a circle, one on a stone, another on the waggon rails, a third on a piece of plank. Gradually the children stole away up the canyon to where there was another chute, somewhat smaller than the one across the dump; and down this chute, for the rest of the afternoon, they poured one avalanche of stones after another, waking the echoes of the glen. Meantime we elders sat together on the platform, Hanson and his friend smoking in silence like Indian sachems, Mrs. Hanson rattling on as usual with an adroit volubility, saying nothing, but keeping the party at their ease like a courtly hostess.

Not a word occurred about the business of the day. Once, twice, and thrice I tried to slide the subject in, but was discouraged by the stoic apathy of Rufe, and beaten down before the pouring verbiage of his wife. There is nothing of the Indian brave about me, and I began to grill with impatience. At last, like a highway robber, I cornered Hanson, and bade him stand and deliver his business. Thereupon he gravely rose, as though to hint that this was not a proper place, nor the subject one suitable for squaws, and I, following his example, led him up the plank into our barrack. There he bestowed himself on a box, and unrolled his papers with fastidious deliberation. There were two sheets of note-paper, and an old mining notice, dated May 30th, 1879, part print, part manuscript, and the latter much obliterated by the rains. It was by this identical piece of paper that the mine had been held last year. For thirteen months it had endured the weather and the change of seasons on a cairn behind the shoulder of the canyon; and it was now my business, spreading it before me on the table, and sitting on a valise, to copy its terms, with some necessary changes, twice over on the two sheets of note-paper. One was then to be placed on the same cairn--a "mound of rocks" the notice put it; and the other to be lodged for registration.

Rufe watched me, silently smoking, till I came to the place for the locator's name at the end of the first copy; and when I proposed that he should sign, I thought I saw a scare in his eye. "I don't think that'll be necessary," he said slowly; "just you write it down." Perhaps this mighty hunter, who was the most active member of the local school board, could not write. There would be nothing strange in that. The constable of Calistoga is, and has been for years, a bed-ridden man, and, if I remember rightly, blind. He had more need of the emoluments than another, it was explained; and it was easy for him to "depytize," with a strong accent on the last. So friendly and so free are popular institutions.

When I had done my scrivening, Hanson strolled out, and addressed Breedlove, "Will you step up here a bit?" and after they had disappeared a little while into the chaparral and madrona thicket, they came back again, minus a notice, and the deed was done. The claim was jumped; a tract of mountain-side, fifteen hundred feet long by six hundred wide, with all the earth's precious bowels, had passed from Ronalds to Hanson, and, in the passage, changed its name from the "Mammoth" to the "Calistoga." I had tried to get Rufe to call it after his wife, after himself, and after Garfield, the Republican Presidential candidate of the hour--since then elected, and, alas! dead--but all was in vain. The claim had once been called the Calistoga before, and he seemed to feel safety in returning to that.

And so the history of that mine became once more plunged in darkness, lit only by some monster pyrotechnical displays of gossip. And perhaps the most curious feature of the whole matter is this: that we should have dwelt in this quiet corner of the mountains, with not a dozen neighbours, and yet struggled all the while, like desperate swimmers, in this sea of falsities and contradictions. Wherever a man is, there will be a lie.

TOILS AND PLEASURES

I must try to convey some notion of our life, of how the days passed and what pleasure we took in them, of what there was to do and how we set about doing it, in our mountain hermitage. The house, after we had repaired the worst of the damages, and filled in some of the doors and windows with white cotton cloth, became a healthy and a pleasant dwelling-place, always airy and dry, and haunted by the outdoor perfumes of the glen. Within, it had the look of habitation, the human look. You had only to go into the third room, which we did not use, and see its stones, its sifting earth, its tumbled litter; and then return to our lodging, with the beds made, the plates on the rack, the pail of bright water behind the door, the stove crackling in a corner, and perhaps the table roughly laid against a meal,--and man's order, the little clean spots that he creates to dwell in, were at once contrasted with the rich passivity of nature. And yet our house was everywhere so wrecked and shattered, the air came and went so freely, the sun found so many portholes, the golden outdoor glow shone in so many open chinks, that we enjoyed, at the same time, some of the comforts of a roof and much of the gaiety and brightness of al fresco life. A single shower of rain, to be sure, and we should have been drowned out like mice. But ours was a Californian summer, and an earthquake was a far likelier accident than a shower of rain.

Trustful in this fine weather, we kept the house for kitchen and bedroom, and used the platform as our summer parlour. The sense of privacy, as I have said already, was complete. We could look over the clump on miles of forest and rough hilltop; our eyes commanded some of Napa Valley, where the train ran, and the little country townships sat so close together along the line of the rail. But here there was no man to intrude. None but the Hansons were our visitors. Even they came but at long intervals, or twice daily, at a stated hour, with milk. So our days, as they were never interrupted, drew out to the greater length; hour melted insensibly into hour; the household duties, though they were many, and some of them laborious, dwindled into mere islets of business in a sea of sunny day-time; and it appears to me, looking back, as though the far greater part of our life at Silverado had been passed, propped upon an elbow, or seated on a plank, listening to the silence that there is among the hills.

My work, it is true, was over early in the morning. I rose before any one else, lit the stove, put on the water to boil, and strolled forth upon the platform to wait till it was ready. Silverado would then be still in shadow, the sun shining on the mountain higher up. A clean smell of trees, a smell of the earth at morning, hung in the air. Regularly, every day, there was a single bird, not singing, but awkwardly chirruping among the green madronas, and the sound was cheerful, natural, and stirring. It did not hold the attention, nor interrupt the thread of meditation, like a blackbird or a nightingale; it was mere woodland prattle, of which the mind was conscious like a perfume. The freshness of these morning seasons remained with me far on into the day.

As soon as the kettle boiled, I made porridge and coffee; and that, beyond the literal drawing of water, and the preparation of kindling, which it would be hyperbolical to call the hewing of wood, ended my domestic duties for the day. Thenceforth my wife laboured single-handed in the palace, and I lay or wandered on the platform at my own sweet will. The little corner near the forge, where we found a refuge under the madronas from the unsparing early sun, is indeed connected in my mind with some nightmare encounters over Euclid, and the Latin Grammar. These were known as Sam's lessons. He was supposed to be the victim and the sufferer; but here there must have been some misconception, for whereas I generally retired to bed after one of these engagements, he was no sooner set free than he dashed up to the Chinaman's house, where he had installed a printing press, that great element of civilization, and the sound of his labours would be faintly audible about the canyon half the day.

To walk at all was a laborious business; the foot sank and slid, the boots were cut to pieces, among sharp, uneven, rolling stones. When we crossed the platform in any direction, it was usual to lay a course, following as much as possible the line of waggon rails. Thus, if water were to be drawn, the water-carrier left the house along some tilting planks that we had laid down, and not laid down very well. These carried him to that great highroad, the railway; and the railway served him as far as to the head of the shaft. But from thence to the spring and back again he made the best of his unaided way, staggering among the stones, and wading in low growth of the calcanthus, where the rattlesnakes lay hissing at his passage. Yet I liked to draw water. It was pleasant to dip the gray metal pail into the clean, colourless, cool water; pleasant to carry it back, with the water ripping at the edge, and a broken sunbeam quivering in the midst.

But the extreme roughness of the walking confined us in common practice to the platform, and indeed to those parts of it that were most easily accessible along the line of rails. The rails came straight forward from the shaft, here and there overgrown with little green bushes, but still entire, and still carrying a truck, which it was Sam's delight to trundle to and fro by the hour with various ladings. About midway down the platform, the railroad trended to the right, leaving our house and coasting along the far side within a few yards of the madronas and the forge, and not far of the latter, ended in a sort of platform on the edge of the dump. There, in old days, the trucks were tipped, and their load sent thundering down the chute. There, besides, was the only spot where we could approach the margin of the dump. Anywhere else, you took your life in your right hand when you came within a yard and a half to peer over. For at any moment the dump might begin to slide and carry you down and bury you below its ruins. Indeed, the neighbourhood of an old mine is a place beset with dangers. For as still as Silverado was, at any moment the report of rotten wood might tell us that the platform had fallen into the shaft; the dump might begin to pour into the road below; or a wedge slip in the great upright seam, and hundreds of tons of mountain bury the scene of our encampment.

I have already compared the dump to a rampart, built certainly by some rude people, and for prehistoric wars. It was likewise a frontier. All below was green and woodland, the tall pines soaring one above another, each with a firm outline and full spread of bough. All above was arid, rocky, and bald. The great spout of broken mineral, that had dammed the canyon up, was a creature of man's handi-work, its material dug out with a pick and powder, and spread by the service of the tracks. But nature herself, in that upper district, seemed to have had an eye to nothing besides mining; and even the natural hill-side was all sliding gravel and precarious boulder. Close at the margin of the well leaves would decay to skeletons and mummies, which at length some stronger gust would carry clear of the canyon and scatter in the subjacent woods. Even moisture and decaying vegetable matter could not, with all nature's alchemy, concoct enough soil to nourish a few poor grasses. It is the same, they say, in the neighbourhood of all silver mines; the nature of that precious rock being stubborn with quartz and poisonous with cinnabar. Both were plenty in our Silverado. The stones sparkled white in the sunshine with quartz; they were all stained red with cinnabar. Here, doubtless, came the Indians of yore to paint their faces for the war-path; and cinnabar, if I remember rightly, was one of the few articles of Indian commerce. Now, Sam had it in his undisturbed possession, to pound down and slake, and paint his rude designs with. But to me it had always a fine flavour of poetry, compounded out of Indian story and Hawthornden's allusion:

"Desire, alas! I desire a Zeuxis new, From Indies borrowing gold, from Eastern skies Most bright cinoper . . ."

Yet this is but half the picture; our Silverado platform has another side to it. Though there was no soil, and scarce a blade of grass, yet out of these tumbled gravel-heaps and broken boulders, a flower garden bloomed as at home in a conservatory. Calcanthus crept, like a hardy weed, all over our rough parlour, choking the railway, and pushing forth its rusty, aromatic cones from between two blocks of shattered mineral. Azaleas made a big snow-bed just above the well. The shoulder of the hill waved white with Mediterranean heath. In the crannies of the ledge and about the spurs of the tall pine, a red flowering stone-plant hung in clusters. Even the low, thorny chaparral was thick with pea-like blossom. Close at the foot of our path nutmegs prospered, delightful to the sight and smell. At sunrise, and again late at night, the scent of the sweet bay trees filled the canyon, and the down-blowing night wind must have borne it hundreds of feet into the outer air.

All this vegetation, to be sure, was stunted. The madrona was here no bigger than the manzanita; the bay was but a stripling shrub; the very pines, with four or five exceptions in all our upper canyon, were not so tall as myself, or but a little taller, and the most of them came lower than my waist. For a prosperous forest tree, we must look below, where the glen was crowded with green spires. But for flowers and ravishing perfume, we had none to envy: our heap of road-metal was thick with bloom, like a hawthorn in the front of June; our red, baking angle in the mountain, a laboratory of poignant scents. It was an endless wonder to my mind, as I dreamed about the platform, following the progress of the shadows, where the madrona with its leaves, the azalea and calcanthus with their blossoms, could find moisture to support such thick, wet, waxy growths, or the bay tree collect the ingredients of its perfume. But there they all grew together, healthy, happy, and happy-making, as though rooted in a fathom of black soil.

Nor was it only vegetable life that prospered. We had, indeed, few birds, and none that had much of a voice or anything worthy to be called a song. My morning comrade had a thin chirp, unmusical and monotonous, but friendly and pleasant to hear. He had but one rival: a fellow with an ostentatious cry of near an octave descending, not one note of which properly followed another. This is the only bird I ever knew with a wrong ear; but there was something enthralling about his performance. You listened and listened, thinking each time he must surely get it right; but no, it was always wrong, and always wrong the same way. Yet he seemed proud of his song, delivered it with execution and a manner of his own, and was charming to his mate. A very incorrect, incessant human whistler had thus a chance of knowing how his own music pleased the world. Two great birds--eagles, we thought-- dwelt at the top of the canyon, among the crags that were printed on the sky. Now and again, but very rarely, they wheeled high over our heads in silence, or with a distant, dying scream; and then, with a fresh impulse, winged fleetly forward, dipped over a hilltop, and were gone. They seemed solemn and ancient things, sailing the blue air: perhaps co-oeval with the mountain where they haunted, perhaps emigrants from Rome, where the glad legions may have shouted to behold them on the morn of battle.

But if birds were rare, the place abounded with rattlesnakes--the rattlesnake's nest, it might have been named. Wherever we brushed among the bushes, our passage woke their angry buzz. One dwelt habitually in the wood-pile, and sometimes, when we came for firewood, thrust up his small head between two logs, and hissed at the intrusion. The rattle has a legendary credit; it is said to be awe-inspiring, and, once heard, to stamp itself for ever in the memory. But the sound is not at all alarming; the hum of many insects, and the buzz of the wasp convince the ear of danger quite as readily. As a matter of fact, we lived for weeks in Silverado, coming and going, with rattles sprung on every side, and it never occurred to us to be afraid. I used to take sun-baths and do calisthenics in a certain pleasant nook among azalea and calcanthus, the rattles whizzing on every side like spinning- wheels, and the combined hiss or buzz rising louder and angrier at any sudden movement; but I was never in the least impressed, nor ever attacked. It was only towards the end of our stay, that a man down at Calistoga, who was expatiating on the terrifying nature of the sound, gave me at last a very good imitation; and it burst on me at once that we dwelt in the very metropolis of deadly snakes, and that the rattle was simply the commonest noise in Silverado. Immediately on our return, we attacked the Hansons on the subject. They had formerly assured us that our canyon was favoured, like Ireland, with an entire immunity from poisonous reptiles; but, with the perfect inconsequence of the natural man, they were no sooner found out than they went off at score in the contrary direction, and we were told that in no part of the world did rattlesnakes attain to such a monstrous bigness as among the warm, flower-dotted rocks of Silverado. This is a contribution rather to the natural history of the Hansons, than to that of snakes.

One person, however, better served by his instinct, had known the rattle from the first; and that was Chuchu, the dog. No rational creature has ever led an existence more poisoned by terror than that dog's at Silverado. Every whiz of the rattle made him bound. His eyes rolled; he trembled; he would be often wet with sweat. One of our great mysteries was his terror of the mountain. A little away above our nook, the azaleas and almost all the vegetation ceased. Dwarf pines not big enough to be Christmas trees, grew thinly among loose stone and gravel scaurs. Here and there a big boulder sat quiescent on a knoll, having paused there till the next rain in his long slide down the mountain. There was here no ambuscade for the snakes, you could see clearly where you trod; and yet the higher I went, the more abject and appealing became Chuchu's terror. He was an excellent master of that composite language in which dogs communicate with men, and he would assure me, on his honour, that there was some peril on the mountain; appeal to me, by all that I held holy, to turn back; and at length, finding all was in vain, and that I still persisted, ignorantly foolhardy, he would suddenly whip round and make a bee- line down the slope for Silverado, the gravel showering after him. What was he afraid of? There were admittedly brown bears and California lions on the mountain; and a grizzly visited Rufe's poultry yard not long before, to the unspeakable alarm of Caliban, who dashed out to chastise the intruder, and found himself, by moonlight, face to face with such a tartar. Something at least there must have been: some hairy, dangerous brute lodged permanently among the rocks a little to the north-west of Silverado, spending his summer thereabout, with wife and family.

And there was, or there had been, another animal. Once, under the broad daylight, on that open stony hillside, where the baby pines were growing, scarcely tall enough to be a badge for a MacGregor's bonnet, I came suddenly upon his innocent body, lying mummified by the dry air and sun: a pigmy kangaroo. I am ingloriously ignorant of these subjects; had never heard of such a beast; thought myself face to face with some incomparable sport of nature; and began to cherish hopes of immortality in science. Rarely have I been conscious of a stranger thrill than when I raised that singular creature from the stones, dry as a board, his innocent heart long quiet, and all warm with sunshine. His long hind legs were stiff, his tiny forepaws clutched upon his breast, as if to leap; his poor life cut short upon that mountain by some unknown accident. But the kangaroo rat, it proved, was no such unknown animal; and my discovery was nothing.

Crickets were not wanting. I thought I could make out exactly four of them, each with a corner of his own, who used to make night musical at Silverado. In the matter of voice, they far excelled the birds, and their ringing whistle sounded from rock to rock, calling and replying the same thing, as in a meaningless opera. Thus, children in full health and spirits shout together, to the dismay of neighbours; and their idle, happy, deafening vociferations rise and fall, like the song of the crickets. I used to sit at night on the platform, and wonder why these creatures were so happy; and what was wrong with man that he also did not wind up his days with an hour or two of shouting; but I suspect that all long-lived animals are solemn. The dogs alone are hardly used by nature; and it seems a manifest injustice for poor Chuchu to die in his teens, after a life so shadowed and troubled, continually shaken with alarm, and the tear of elegant sentiment permanently in his eye.

There was another neighbour of ours at Silverado, small but very active, a destructive fellow. This was a black, ugly fly--a bore, the Hansons called him--who lived by hundreds in the boarding of our house. He entered by a round hole, more neatly pierced than a man could do it with a gimlet, and he seems to have spent his life in cutting out the interior of the plank, but whether as a dwelling or a storehouse, I could never find. When I used to lie in bed in the morning for a rest--we had no easy-chairs in Silverado--I would hear, hour after hour, the sharp cutting sound of his labours, and from time to time a dainty shower of sawdust would fall upon the blankets. There lives no more industrious creature than a bore.

And now that I have named to the reader all our animals and insects without exception--only I find I have forgotten the flies--he will be able to appreciate the singular privacy and silence of our days. It was not only man who was excluded: animals, the song of birds, the lowing of cattle, the bleating of sheep, clouds even, and the variations of the weather, were here also wanting; and as, day after day, the sky was one dome of blue, and the pines below us stood motionless in the still air, so the hours themselves were marked out from each other only by the series of our own affairs, and the sun's great period as he ranged westward through the heavens. The two birds cackled a while in the early morning; all day the water tinkled in the shaft, the bores ground sawdust in the planking of our crazy palace--infinitesimal sounds; and it was only with the return of night that any change would fall on our surroundings, or the four crickets begin to flute together in the dark.

Indeed, it would be hard to exaggerate the pleasure that we took in the approach of evening. Our day was not very long, but it was very tiring. To trip along unsteady planks or wade among shifting stones, to go to and fro for water, to clamber down the glen to the Toll House after meat and letters, to cook, to make fires and beds, were all exhausting to the body. Life out of doors, besides, under the fierce eye of day, draws largely on the animal spirits. There are certain hours in the afternoon when a man, unless he is in strong health or enjoys a vacant mind, would rather creep into a cool corner of a house and sit upon the chairs of civilization. About that time, the sharp stones, the planks, the upturned boxes of Silverado, began to grow irksome to my body; I set out on that hopeless, never-ending quest for a more comfortable posture; I would be fevered and weary of the staring sun; and just then he would begin courteously to withdraw his countenance, the shadows lengthened, the aromatic airs awoke, and an indescribable but happy change announced the coming of the night.

The hours of evening, when we were once curtained in the friendly dark, sped lightly. Even as with the crickets, night brought to us a certain spirit of rejoicing. It was good to taste the air; good to mark the dawning of the stars, as they increased their glittering company; good, too, to gather stones, and send them crashing down the chute, a wave of light. It seemed, in some way, the reward and the fulfilment of the day. So it is when men dwell in the open air; it is one of the simple pleasures that we lose by living cribbed and covered in a house, that, though the coming of the day is still the most inspiriting, yet day's departure, also, and the return of night refresh, renew, and quiet us; and in the pastures of the dusk we stand, like cattle, exulting in the absence of the load.

Our nights wore never cold, and they were always still, but for one remarkable exception. Regularly, about nine o'clock, a warm wind sprang up, and blew for ten minutes, or maybe a quarter of an hour, right down the canyon, fanning it well out, airing it as a mother airs the night nursery before the children sleep. As far as I could judge, in the clear darkness of the night, this wind was purely local: perhaps dependant on the configuration of the glen. At least, it was very welcome to the hot and weary squatters; and if we were not abed already, the springing up of this lilliputian valley-wind would often be our signal to retire.

I was the last to go to bed, as I was still the first to rise. Many a night I have strolled about the platform, taking a bath of darkness before I slept. The rest would be in bed, and even from the forge I could hear them talking together from bunk to bunk. A single candle in the neck of a pint bottle was their only illumination; and yet the old cracked house seemed literally bursting with the light. It shone keen as a knife through all the vertical chinks; it struck upward through the broken shingles; and through the eastern door and window, it fell in a great splash upon the thicket and the overhanging rock. You would have said a conflagration, or at the least a roaring forge; and behold, it was but a candle. Or perhaps it was yet more strange to see the procession moving bedwards round the corner of the house, and up the plank that brought us to the bedroom door; under the immense spread of the starry heavens, down in a crevice of the giant mountain these few human shapes, with their unshielded taper, made so disproportionate a figure in the eye and mind. But the more he is alone with nature, the greater man and his doings bulk in the consideration of his fellow-men. Miles and miles away upon the opposite hill-tops, if there were any hunter belated or any traveller who had lost his way, he must have stood, and watched and wondered, from the time the candle issued from the door of the assayer's office till it had mounted the plank and disappeared again into the miners' dormitory.

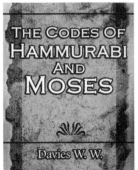

The Codes Of Hammurabi And Moses
W. W. Davies

QTY

The discovery of the Hammurabi Code is one of the greatest achievements of archaeology, and is of paramount interest, not only to the student of the Bible, but also to all those interested in ancient history...

Religion   **ISBN:** *1-59462-338-4*   **Pages:132**
MSRP $12.95

The Theory of Moral Sentiments
Adam Smith

QTY

This work from 1749. contains original theories of conscience amd moral judgment and it is the foundation for systemof morals.

Philosophy **ISBN:** *1-59462-777-0*   **Pages:536**
MSRP $19.95

Jessica's First Prayer
Hesba Stretton

QTY

In a screened and secluded corner of one of the many railway-bridges which span the streets of London there could be seen a few years ago, from five o'clock every morning until half past eight, a tidily set-out coffee-stall, consisting of a trestle and board, upon which stood two large tin cans, with a small fire of charcoal burning under each so as to keep the coffee boiling during the early hours of the morning when the work-people were thronging into the city on their way to their daily toil...

Pages:84

Childrens   **ISBN:** *1-59462-373-2*   *MSRP $9.95*

My Life and Work
Henry Ford

QTY

Henry Ford revolutionized the world with his implementation of mass production for the Model T automobile. Gain valuable business insight into his life and work with his own auto-biography... "We have only started on our development of our country we have not as yet, with all our talk of wonderful progress, done more than scratch the surface. The progress has been wonderful enough but..."

Pages:300

Biographies/   **ISBN:** *1-59462-198-5*   *MSRP $21.95*

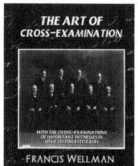

The Art of Cross-Examination
Francis Wellman

QTY

I presume it is the experience of every author, after his first book is published upon an important subject, to be almost overwhelmed with a wealth of ideas and illustrations which could readily have been included in his book, and which to his own mind, at least, seem to make a second edition inevitable. Such certainly was the case with me; and when the first edition had reached its sixth impression in five months, I rejoiced to learn that it seemed to my publishers that the book had met with a sufficiently favorable reception to justify a second and considerably enlarged edition. ..

Pages:412

Reference   ISBN: *1-59462-647-2*   *MSRP $19.95*

On the Duty of Civil Disobedience
Henry David Thoreau

QTY

Thoreau wrote his famous essay, On the Duty of Civil Disobedience, as a protest against an unjust but popular war and the immoral but popular institution of slave-owning. He did more than write—he declined to pay his taxes, and was hauled off to gaol in consequence. Who can say how much this refusal of his hastened the end of the war and of slavery ?

Law   ISBN: *1-59462-747-9*   **Pages:48**

MSRP $7.45

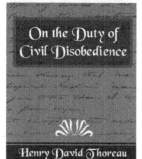

Dream Psychology Psychoanalysis for Beginners
Sigmund Freud

QTY

Sigmund Freud, born Sigismund Schlomo Freud (May 6, 1856 - September 23, 1939), was a Jewish-Austrian neurologist and psychiatrist who co-founded the psychoanalytic school of psychology. Freud is best known for his theories of the unconscious mind, especially involving the mechanism of repression; his redefinition of sexual desire as mobile and directed towards a wide variety of objects; and his therapeutic techniques, especially his understanding of transference in the therapeutic relationship and the presumed value of dreams as sources of insight into unconscious desires.

Pages:196

Psychology   ISBN: *1-59462-905-6*   *MSRP $15.45*

The Miracle of Right Thought
Orison Swett Marden

QTY

Believe with all of your heart that you will do what you were made to do. When the mind has once formed the habit of holding cheerful, happy, prosperous pictures, it will not be easy to form the opposite habit. It does not matter how improbable or how far away this realization may see, or how dark the prospects may be, if we visualize them as best we can, as vividly as possible, hold tenaciously to them and vigorously struggle to attain them, they will gradually become actualized, realized in the life. But a desire, a longing without endeavor, a yearning abandoned or held indifferently will vanish without realization.

Pages:360

Self Help   ISBN: *1-59462-644-8*   *MSRP $25.45*

QTY

The Rosicrucian Cosmo-Conception Mystic Christianity by *Max Heindel* ISBN: *1-59462-188-8* **$38.95**
The Rosicrucian Cosmo-conception is not dogmatic, neither does it appeal to any other authority than the reason of the student. It is: not controversial, but is: sent forth in the, hope that it may help to clear... New Age/Religion Pages 646

Abandonment To Divine Providence by *Jean-Pierre de Caussade* ISBN: *1-59462-228-0* **$25.95**
"The Rev. Jean Pierre de Caussade was one of the most remarkable spiritual writers of the Society of Jesus in France in the 18th Century. His death took place at Toulouse in 1751. His works have gone through many editions and have been republished... Inspirational/Religion Pages 400

Mental Chemistry by *Charles Haanel* ISBN: *1-59462-192-6* **$23.95**
Mental Chemistry allows the change of material conditions by combining and appropriately utilizing the power of the mind. Much like applied chemistry creates something new and unique out of careful combinations of chemicals the mastery of mental chemistry... New Age Pages 354

The Letters of Robert Browning and Elizabeth Barret Barrett 1845-1846 vol II ISBN: *1-59462-193-4* **$35.95**
by *Robert Browning* and *Elizabeth Barrett* Biographies Pages 596

Gleanings In Genesis (volume I) by *Arthur W. Pink* ISBN: *1-59462-130-6* **$27.45**
Appropriately has Genesis been termed "the seed plot of the Bible" for in it we have, in germ form, almost all of the great doctrines which are afterwards fully developed in the books of Scripture which follow... Religion/Inspirational Pages 420

The Master Key by *L. W. de Laurence* ISBN: *1-59462-001-6* **$30.95**
In no branch of human knowledge has there been a more lively increase of the spirit of research during the past few years than in the study of Psychology, Concentration and Mental Discipline. The requests for authentic lessons in Thought Control, Mental Discipline and... New Age/Business Pages 422

The Lesser Key Of Solomon Goetia by *L. W. de Laurence* ISBN: *1-59462-092-X* **$9.95**
This translation of the first book of the "Lernegton" which is now for the first time made accessible to students of Talismanic Magic was done, after careful collation and edition, from numerous Ancient Manuscripts in Hebrew, Latin, and French... New Age/Occult Pages 92

Rubaiyat Of Omar Khayyam by *Edward Fitzgerald* ISBN:*1-59462-332-5* **$13.95**
Edward Fitzgerald, whom the world has already learned, in spite of his own efforts to remain within the shadow of anonymity, to look upon as one of the rarest poets of the century, was born at Bredfield, in Suffolk, on the 31st of March, 1809. He was the third son of John Purcell... Music Pages 172

Ancient Law by *Henry Maine* ISBN: *1-59462-128-4* **$29.95**
The chief object of the following pages is to indicate some of the earliest ideas of mankind, as they are reflected in Ancient Law, and to point out the relation of those ideas to modern thought. Religion/History Pages 452

Far-Away Stories by *William J. Locke* ISBN: *1-59462-129-2* **$19.45**
"Good wine needs no bush, but a collection of mixed vintages does. And this book is just such a collection. Some of the stories I do not want to remain buried for ever in the museum files of dead magazine-numbers an author's not unpardonable vanity..." Fiction Pages 272

Life of David Crockett by *David Crockett* ISBN: *1-59462-250-7* **$27.45**
"Colonel David Crockett was one of the most remarkable men of the times in which he lived. Born in humble life, but gifted with a strong will, an indomitable courage, and unremitting perseverance... Biographies/New Age Pages 424

Lip-Reading by *Edward Nitchie* ISBN: *1-59462-206-X* **$25.95**
Edward B. Nitchie, founder of the New York School for the Hard of Hearing, now the Nitchie School of Lip-Reading, Inc, wrote "LIP-READING Principles and Practice". The development and perfecting of this meritorious work on lip-reading was an undertaking... How-to Pages 400

A Handbook of Suggestive Therapeutics, Applied Hypnotism, Psychic Science ISBN: *1-59462-214-0* **$24.95**
by *Henry Munro* Health/New Age/Health/Self-help Pages 376

A Doll's House: and Two Other Plays by *Henrik Ibsen* ISBN: *1-59462-112-8* **$19.95**
Henrik Ibsen created this classic when in revolutionary 1848 Rome. Introducing some striking concepts in playwriting for the realist genre, this play has been studied the world over. Fiction/Classics/Plays 308

The Light of Asia by *sir Edwin Arnold* ISBN: *1-59462-204-3* **$13.95**
In this poetic masterpiece, Edwin Arnold describes the life and teachings of Buddha. The man who was to become known as Buddha to the world was born as Prince Gautama of India but he rejected the worldly riches and abandoned the reigns of power when... Religion/History/Biographies Pages 170

The Complete Works of Guy de Maupassant by *Guy de Maupassant* ISBN: *1-59462-157-8* **$16.95**
"For days and days, nights and nights, I had dreamed of that first kiss which was to consecrate our engagement, and I knew not on what spot I should put my lips..." Fiction/Classics Pages 240

The Art of Cross-Examination by *Francis L. Wellman* ISBN: *1-59462-309-0* **$26.95**
Written by a renowned trial lawyer, Wellman imparts his experience and uses case studies to explain how to use psychology to extract desired information through questioning. How-to/Science/Reference Pages 408

Answered or Unanswered? by *Louisa Vaughan* ISBN: *1-59462-248-5* **$10.95**
Miracles of Faith in China Religion Pages 112

The Edinburgh Lectures on Mental Science (1909) by *Thomas* ISBN: *1-59462-008-3* **$11.95**
This book contains the substance of a course of lectures recently given by the writer in the Queen Street Hall, Edinburgh. Its purpose is to indicate the Natural Principles governing the relation between Mental Action and Material Conditions... New Age/Psychology Pages 148

Ayesha by *H. Rider Haggard* ISBN: *1-59462-301-5* **$24.95**
Verily and indeed it is the unexpected that happens! Probably if there was one person upon the earth from whom the Editor of this, and of a certain previous history, did not expect to hear again... Classics Pages 380

Ayala's Angel by *Anthony Trollope* ISBN: *1-59462-352-X* **$29.95**
The two girls were both pretty, but Lucy who was twenty-one who supposed to be simple and comparatively unattractive, whereas Ayala was credited, as her Bombwhat romantic name might show, with poetic charm and a taste for romance. Ayala when her father died was nineteen... Fiction Pages 484

The American Commonwealth by *James Bryce* ISBN: *1-59462-286-8* **$34.45**
An interpretation of American democratic political theory. It examines political mechanics and society from the perspective of Scotsman James Bryce Politics Pages 572

Stories of the Pilgrims by *Margaret P. Pumphrey* ISBN: *1-59462-116-0* **$17.95**
This book explores pilgrims religious oppression in England as well as their escape to Holland and eventual crossing to America on the Mayflower, and their early days in New England... History Pages 268

QTY

The Fasting Cure by *Sinclair Upton*   ISBN: *1-59462-222-1* **$13.95**
In the Cosmopolitan Magazine for May, 1910, and in the Contemporary Review (London) for April, 1910, I published an article dealing with my experiences in fasting. I have written a great many magazine articles, but never one which attracted so much attention... New Age/Self Help/Health Pages 164

Hebrew Astrology by *Sepharial*   ISBN: *1-59462-308-2* **$13.45**
In these days of advanced thinking it is a matter of common observation that we have left many of the old landmarks behind and that we are now pressing forward to greater heights and to a wider horizon than that which represented the mind-content of our progenitors... Astrology Pages 144

Thought Vibration or The Law of Attraction in the Thought World   ISBN: *1-59462-127-6* **$12.95**
by *William Walker Atkinson*   Psychology/Religion Pages 144

Optimism by *Helen Keller*   ISBN: *1-59462-108-X* **$15.95**
Helen Keller was blind, deaf, and mute since 19 months old, yet famously learned how to overcome these handicaps, communicate with the world, and spread her lectures promoting optimism. An inspiring read for everyone... Biographies/Inspirational Pages 84

Sara Crewe by *Frances Burnett*   ISBN: *1-59462-360-0* **$9.45**
In the first place, Miss Minchin lived in London. Her home was a large, dull, tall one, in a large, dull square, where all the houses were alike, and all the sparrows were alike, and where all the door-knockers made the same heavy sound... Childrens Classic Pages 88

The Autobiography of Benjamin Franklin by *Benjamin Franklin*   ISBN: *1-59462-135-7* **$24.95**
The Autobiography of Benjamin Franklin has probably been more extensively read than any other American historical work, and no other book of its kind has had such ups and downs of fortune. Franklin lived for many years in England, where he was agent... Biographies/History Pages 332

Name	
Email	
Telephone	
Address	
City, State ZIP	

☐ **Credit Card**   ☐ **Check / Money Order**

Credit Card Number	
Expiration Date	
Signature	

Please Mail to: Book Jungle
                   PO Box 2226
                   Champaign, IL 61825
or Fax to: 630-214-0564

ORDERING INFORMATION

web*: www.bookjungle.com*
email*: sales@bookjungle.com*
fax*: 630-214-0564*
mail*: Book Jungle PO Box 2226 Champaign, IL 61825*
or PayPal *to sales@bookjungle.com*

Please contact us for bulk discounts

DIRECT-ORDER TERMS

**20% Discount if You Order
Two or More Books**
Free Domestic Shipping!
Accepted: Master Card, Visa,
Discover, American Express